A PATHWAY THROUGH PAIN

Also by Jane Grayshon:

Treasures of Darkness
In Times of Pain
Faith in Flames
Confessions of a Vicar's Wife
Vicar's Wife on the Move

A Pathway Through Pain

Revised and updated

JANE GRAYSHON

MONARCH
BOOKS

Mill Hill, London & Grand Rapids, Michigan

This edition published by Monarch Books in the UK 2002,
Concorde House, Grenville Place,
Mill Hill, London NW7 3SA.

Distributed by:
UK: STL, PO Box 300, Kingstown Broadway, Carlisle,
Cumbria CA3 0QS;
USA: Kregel Publications, PO Box 2607,
Grand Rapids, Michigan 49501.

ISBN 1 85424 581 3

British Library Cataloguing Data
A catalogue record for this book is available
from the British Library.

Book design and production for the publishers by
Bookprint Creative Services
P.O. Box 827, BN21 3YJ, England
Printed in Great Britain.

To all those who are hurting
somewhere inside

"Your path led through the sea,
your way through the mighty waters,
though your footprints were not seen."

Psalm 77:19

CONTENTS

INTRODUCTION TO THIRD EDITION

Since this book was first published fifteen years ago I have received a constant stream of letters. People have written not just to express gratitude but, more significantly, to share a resounding sense of relief. "Thank you for putting into words what I couldn't say for myself but desperately needed to share!"

That is why I wrote this book. I am convinced that, even though we find it hard to say so, most of us have experienced moments of darkness, of feeling that prayer doesn't seem to be working properly for us. Many assume that they have "too little faith", at least in the church's eyes. Some also feel condemned by God; in their disappointment and disillusionment they let go of even the thin thread of faith they may have had.

There are many books about Christians who prayed and were miraculously healed; there are others about those who prayed and died heroically. Both give glory to God. They are thrilling testimonies which encourage us to pay attention to how God can act.

My pain hasn't been miraculously healed, nor have I died victoriously. This story is about praying and not seeing circumstances change. It is about being disappointed in God because he did not do what I wanted and asked him to do. He was not obedient to me. Strangely it was in the acceptance of this reality that I gradually discovered that that made him all the greater. He was God, not me. The sovereignty of God is painful indeed.

While I was preparing to write the text, I found myself turning, almost every morning, to Isaiah, chapter 61. This is a prophecy about the changes Jesus would bring to our lives. Jesus actually quoted these words when he first talked about the purpose of his coming:

> ... the Lord has anointed me
> to preach good news to the poor ...
> to bind up the broken-hearted,
> to proclaim freedom for the captives
> and release ... for the prisoners ...
> to comfort all who mourn ...

Almost every time I read the verses, I sensed a nudge from God. "These are the people you're writing for!"

Thus I have written this book for people who are broken-hearted, captive to their circumstances, or grieving for what they have lost. I have written for those who feel poor emotionally, spiritually, or physically.

The reason I have written it is to convey the good news that the spirit of despair, which naturally falls on us during times of deep suffering, need not stay with us for ever. We cannot shed the despair; neither can we manufacture a garment of praise. The good news is that God can do both – even if he doesn't change our actual circumstances.

I have written it because God doesn't always stop bad things happening. Freedom did not come to me by God removing my pain. The beginning of freedom for me was to accept the fact that it looked as if God had deserted me completely. That was when I began to realize that he is everywhere: even in my (our) sense of abandonment. That was when I first glimpsed that he could be known in a special way *because of* the pain, awful though it was.

This is not a theological essay about "the goodness of God amid suffering". This book is about my search for the goodness of God, about not finding what I was looking for, but finding what I was not expecting.

Meister Eckhardt, a medieval mystic, wrote, "God is like a person who clears his throat while hiding, and so gives himself away." I hope to share, in this book, something of the reality of suffering, and also the reality of God, whose cough we hear and whom we long to meet face to face.

Jane Grayshon

December 2001

PART ONE

Overtaken by Pain

CHAPTER ONE

"LET THIS CUP PASS FROM ME"

Matthew 26:39

Life with three brothers had many challenges for a girl of my personality. Keeping up with them became my determined goal from an early age. It was very important to me that I should learn to survive any masculine teases and to avoid being labelled a sissy. We would all hear about my grandmother and her eight brothers. Those bedtime stories from the family archives served to quicken the challenge I already felt. If she could survive eight brothers, then I would make sure I could keep my end up with just three.

"You can't go up our rope-ladder . . . "

"You couldn't climb to the top of the pear tree . . . "

I would rise to the bait every time. During my earliest years I decided never to give others the opportunity to label me a weakling. I would steel myself against any fear or pain; taking a huge breath, I would climb the disputed pear tree right to the top, navigating the rope-ladder at speed. Inevitably I would disregard such humiliating inconveniences as bleeding knees or my ribbons falling out of my pigtails. On reaching the top I would feel exhilarated, if not by the view across to Liverpool then by the pleasure of proving . . . proving *what*, I ask myself, 40 years on?!

I wonder, now, if I believed I was proving my very worth in life. To be acceptable I felt I had to be brave.

It has not come easily to me, therefore, to discover that there are situations with which I cannot cope. When all my "bravery" was used up I have felt utterly unacceptable not only to others but, perhaps more significantly, to myself.

It has been a rude awakening. Pain became a prominent thread in the tapestry of my life in 1976 when I was only 21, creeping in like an intruder, a thief which stole a part of my very self. It drove me to the point of crying out in anguish, "I can't bear any more!" During five dark months in 1980 I came closest to giving up altogether. I can never adequately describe the totality of my exhaustion with illness, with pain, with life itself.

Matthew, my husband, and I had moved to Nottingham in order for him to step from teacher to student, his aim being to qualify for ministry in the Church of England. We had adjusted from the very different life we had been living in Edinburgh, where Matthew had been a schoolteacher and I had graduated as a nurse. Although that change had been a major decision, it was made easier by the fact that we shared our Christian faith and had already tasted the enjoyment of leading things together, for example, the church youth group (well, it was a group of over-20s, actually, but I now call that "youth"!). During Matthew's four years at theological college in Nottingham, I was the breadwinner and, by 1980, I'd been promoted to a job I absolutely loved. I was a research sister, working both clinically and academically in the field of midwifery. Anyone but the closest observer would have described my life as looking very good – until early 1980.

In the February, when that crisis began, I was already profoundly weary from four years of chronic low-level pain resulting from the severe peritonitis that had heralded the start of all this illness. Though I knew it was normal for me,

I still winced every time I moved too vigorously and felt the heavy ache. Painkillers were either not strong enough or they caused me to feel sick. In any case, I tended not to take them as I feared that they would lose their effect if I took them too often. I dreaded having nothing to fall back on.

Pain began to be an unwelcome part of every conversation: so much so that I would secretly think, I hope this finishes soon; I need to rest quietly. Yet I couldn't rest, for the pain made me restless. And if I *were* left to be quiet, I would yearn for conversation to distract me. Neither I nor my caring friends could win. There was no remedy. I easily became irritable, which in turn made me yet more irritable because I knew I was being short-tempered and I hated myself for it.

On top of this chronic situation, acute pain broke in. At first I thought I was pregnant. For two weeks my spirits rose, only dampened by the extra tiredness. But as the pain increased, my excitement faded. My experience of a few years as a midwife told me that the symptoms I was experiencing were ominous.

Somehow I managed to keep working. I cared for several patients who were complaining of pain, but in my heart I began to become hardened against any who did not seem genuine. I remember catching a glimpse of one such girl who typified exactly the kind of patient whom I didn't want to be. One moment she was giggling with her boyfriend in the waiting-room, but as soon as she reached the consulting room she looked very sorry for herself and moaned dramatically about the "terrible pain, Doctor". Perhaps I was being harsh or judgemental, but she seemed to be making a big fuss about very little, while I was trying desperately to make no fuss – about something! I was tempted to say to anyone who didn't seem genuinely ill, "You've no idea what terrible pain is if you can giggle through it." But I did not speak. One of the doctors for whom I worked was Richard, my own consultant. I was not ready to talk about myself – least of all to him. I suppose one half of me knew all too well what he might find if he examined me. I was afraid: afraid of being told I was not achieving my childhood aim of being brave.

Thus I kept going. Every evening I would drive home along the foggy Nottingham roads and just flop into bed. Matthew was working so hard at theological college, training for full-time ministry, that he did not see how much time I spent in bed. He ate his meals in the theological college, so he didn't realize how little I was eating. At night he was so tired, he would sleep soundly through my hours spent vainly trying to find a comfortable position in which to sleep.

On one particular Tuesday in that February I found myself quite unable to walk briskly around the wards. I had to collect a blood sample for research from a patient in labour. I remember the other midwife beside me who was so comforting towards our patient. I found myself wishing that I were on the receiving end of such comfort. Instead I had to whip myself simply to keep going, keep going . . .

In everything I did, I had to give myself instructions:

Walk over to pick up a syringe and needle. Force yourself. Walk over there. Keep upright.

Keep walking down this corridor. You can do it.

Smile to that lady. Make your eyes smile as well, so that she doesn't perceive how much pain you're in.

The fighting part of my nature was determined not to give in. One part of me hoped that, if I ignored the pain, it might all just resolve itself. However, another part of me, more deeply buried, longed for someone, somehow, to perceive the agony I was in and ask me about it. I was caught between the fear of how ill I might be, and a different fear of crumpling into tears like a silly child.

On the Wednesday, I had to help with some medical

students' exams. Normally I loved that, for I mercilessly teased all the consultants and professors who conducted the exams. I liked to pull them down a peg or two because of the pompous stance they all assumed to terrify the medics. (They in their turn were so bored with examining, they enjoyed a bit of banter.)

But that Wednesday I was very subdued. At the end of the morning session, Richard was missing my usual drama and singing.

"You all right?" he asked discreetly as we walked across an enclosed bridge for lunch. The door at the end was open, revealing tables laden with delicious food; girls in starched white hats stood ready to serve us generously. I thought I might vomit just at the sight of it.

"Not bad," I mumbled in reply. I was careful for my eyes not to meet his. My fear of crumpling was greater than the longing for appropriate care, diagnosis and treatment.

"It's red for you, isn't it?" He gestured to the dozens of bottles of expensive wine. "Oh look, they've even got your favourite: St Emilion."

"No thanks, Richard. Er, I don't think I will today." Richard looked at me incredulously and, for the first time, I dared to meet his gaze.

Summoning all my courage, I managed to splutter out a minimum of words. "I think perhaps I need some anti-biotics."

There. I'd said it. Surely I could be pleased with myself! And I could tell Matthew later that I had "confessed", and he would be pleased and relieved. A few antibiotics would clear everything up. Wouldn't they?

Richard looked at me questioningly for a minute; then, needing to be involved with the other consultants and pro-fessors exchanging news of their recent researches, he agreed. "OK. Get a 'script and I'll sign it." He poured him-self a full glass of Beaujolais nouveau.

I slipped quietly out of the room. By now my abdomen felt as if it were on fire. I knew I should not have appeared so calm and composed in front of Richard. I should have asked him at a more appropriate time when he could have examined me properly. He always trusted me to be honest, and this time I had deliberately masked the true pain and made his job difficult. My wretched fear of being considered silly had dominated. Never mind, I consoled myself. The antibiotics will soon work.

The afternoon passed. I longed to lie down or even to lean over a table and rest my head and my tummy. After he'd signed the prescription Richard looked up.

"You shouldn't be here," he said, his tone more sombre this time. "Get home and start chewing these." He added a request for a huge bottle of strong painkillers. "You won't take these all at once, will you?" He laughed heartily at his joke. I gave a rather distant smile. I did not laugh, because even the muscular movement of laughter would cause the pain to sear through me. In any case, perhaps it wasn't such a joke. I was beginning to feel as if I couldn't bear this much longer.

I did not go straight home. I went to my office and wrote up all the outstanding reports, dealt with all correspondence and tidied my files. I think I must have sensed that I would not be there again for a long time. I didn't want to leave until I knew everything was ordered and up to date.

I spent the following days in bed. Matthew's face became more and more anxious, though he kept trying to cheer me up whenever he brought me drinks. Every time he had to remove a tray of food I hadn't managed to eat, his face set a little more. He knew I was getting worse, but neither of us wanted to be the first to say so.

Two or three times we had to call the local doctor to see me. Once was on the Saturday evening and the doctor-on-call who came seemed so hard-pressed he appeared to resent having had to visit me at all.

"What can I do for you?" he asked curtly, getting out his prescription pad and flicking his ball-point pen, ready to write.

Matthew replied on my behalf, trying to save me from having to repeat my medical history. "Well, four years ago she had her appendix out and since then . . . " he began.

"I am asking, what is the problem NOW?" The doctor twisted his pen impatiently, waiting to write.

I began to feel agitated. How could we avoid putting my present symptoms into the context of the last few years? This was no isolated dose of flu. I had not been completely healthy for the previous four years, since, a few weeks after my appendix was removed in Edinburgh, an undiagnosed abscess had burst. It had poured its offensive, bug-ridden contents diffusely into my abdomen. Despite rigorous treatment both by surgery and by high doses of antibiotics, the resultant highly infectious micro-organisms had never been completely eradicated. Every so often, the inflammation had reared its ugly head – as again now – each time bringing further debilitating illness and the possibility of serious complications.

How could I summarize all that in one sentence? Especially when the doctor sounded so pressured and we felt so defensive.

I was thankful that Matthew was acting as spokesman for me, because his calm manner gave me confidence in him. On the other hand, he didn't know the language of the medical world and I wondered if I shouldn't step in with some medical terms in order to try to help the doctor understand. I decided that I must intervene if we were to be helped at all.

"I've had pelvic inflammatory disease ever since, with acute bouts of peritonitis intermittently. It seems to have flared up again now. I'm very sore."

"Any pyrexia?"

"No, but my temperature hardly ever goes up, even when I had the first abscess. That's why it wasn't diagnosed, I think . . . "

The doctor had stopped listening as soon as I said "No", and was back to poising his pen over the prescription pad. I was hoping, desperately, that I would enable him to change from his (apparently) train-track line of thought. Clearly, however, I was failing miserably.

"No pyrexia. Well, there's nothing seriously wrong then. I could give you some antibiotics if you really want." He seemed pleased to be able to write something at last.

I looked helplessly towards Matthew. He often goes quiet when there's lots to say: he needs to sift through the thoughts clamouring in his mind before replying. He stood thoughtfully, then his eyes met mine. I could see that he felt unable to argue against that great barrier, the medical profession. I felt frustrated and annoyed that doctors can set themselves up as if their opinion cannot be disputed.

Fortunately I was not left without an argument. "Thank you for the prescription but actually I've been on antibiotics since Wednesday."

"Oh?" He was slightly put off his stride, at least. "Well, they should be doing the trick."

"But they aren't and it's three and a half days now. I'm getting worse, not better. That's why we called you. And I feel so nauseated I can hardly take them."

He snapped his smart doctor's bag shut, lifted it off his knees and placed it on the floor. "I'd better have a look at your tummy. Where is the pain?"

I pointed to the area over one side, carefully avoiding touching it because it was so tender. He laid his cold hand on the opposite side and gradually worked his way across my abdomen, pressing as if he were securing postage stamps rather than palpating me gently. I pulled my legs up involuntarily and drew a deep breath.

Matthew jumped to my defence. "Do be gentle. She's been through a lot," he pleaded.

"This must be done," was the short reply.

By the time he'd finished, my hands were white from clenching my fists. I could no longer discuss things objectively. Nausea was sweeping over me in great waves but I was too shy to lean over the bowl, especially in front of a man who made me feel so un-comforted. It would serve him right if I were sick on him, I thought uncharitably. But then the pain seared through me once again, round to my back and to the top of my legs. I closed my eyes to try to cope silently. To withdraw into myself became my refuge, lying as if alone and mute. Not until I was in my 40s was I to learn that that "refuge" actually cut me off from the very care I needed and craved.

"I will change the prescription for different antibiotics." The doctor picked up that wretched pad and pen once again. "If there's no improvement by Monday, see your own doctor."

I opened my eyes a little. Matthew looked vaguely relieved. He must have thought this remedy was better than nothing. I could not share his confidence but, for his sake, I would do as I was told. In any case, what alternative did I have?

I mustered the energy to ask about what was bothering me. "I feel so sick, I don't know that I can keep the antibiotics or the painkillers down. Please, could you give me something?" I looked at him pleadingly.

"Here, take this." The doctor rummaged in his black bag once again.

"What is it?" As a nursing sister, I never gave my patients any medicine without explaining what it was or how it worked, and I didn't intend to accept anything without knowing about it either.

"Just take it." He held it out to me and nodded firmly

before mumbling, "You nurses are all the same." His eyes looked past me with little compassion, and inside myself I shrivelled up. I was too weary to refuse. I took it.

After he had gone, everything became a blur. The mysterious pill made my head swim, and it was hard for me to distinguish between what was real and what was only in my mind. My thoughts drifted around, accompanied by the fast throb of my heartbeat, almost like swirling music with a pounding drum in the background.

Matthew came and went, kneeling beside the bed and speaking softly and gently. His care soothed me very much. I was so grateful, it was little cost for me to smile in return. But whenever I closed my eyes I was back in a world of pain. Sometimes I had nasty hallucinations; sometimes I sat bolt upright in bed or leaned over to try to shift the pain. Always I was aware of the nausea and pain.

On Monday morning, neither Matthew nor I had any doubt as to what we should do. After Matthew's brief phone call to an understanding secretary in the department where I worked, I had an appointment to see Richard immediately.

I do not quite know how I got myself together enough to reach that consulting room. I shall never forget how I had to fight. Matthew drove me there, taking immense care to avoid bumps in the road so as not to jolt my tummy. Then the short flight of stairs loomed above me, a daunting hurdle. I had to cling on to the banister for support but somehow I made it independently, refusing Matthew's arm to help me up. Once again my age-old determination, linked to my fear of being labelled a "sissy", was driving me onwards and upwards. I mustn't be weak.

As Matthew held open the door of the department, my terror of what Richard might decide about me was temporarily put to one side. Every thought I had was focused on keeping going.

I was back to programming myself: Walk, Jane. Just get to that chair there and lean on that. Be careful not to look as if you're doing a dramatic mimic of a patient in pain. Don't give any opportunity for others to think you're a fraud. Look normal. Don't stoop with the pain . . .

I have always tormented myself with the fear of making a fuss over "nothing". I think that what began up a pear tree was profoundly reinforced when I was treated as such in Edinburgh when I first became ill in 1976. It was only one doctor, for one week, and he was ultimately proved to have been completely mistaken; but his judgemental, sneering manner hurt so deeply that it echoed on and on. Here is another example of how slow I was to learn to switch off the tape of a hurtful voice playing in my mind. All through 1980 my dread was of being written off as not genuine. Rather than explore that fear, I tried instead to prevent myself from ever, possibly, receiving such an accusation. Consequently I underplayed *everything* so that only a truly caring person – someone compassionate enough to look beneath the surface – could ever perceive how I was feeling. It was a precarious game, keeping others at arm's length when what I craved most of all was tenderness and loving care.

Richard's distinctive step approaching jolted me. He beamed at us cheerfully. I swallowed hard and found a lump in my throat. I let go of Matthew's hand, sensing somewhere, deep down I think, the significance of that gesture. Of how much else was I letting go? My fighting, my pretending that all was better than it was.

"See you down in the room," Richard called to me as he whisked into the secretary's office to pick up my notes.

I set off walking ahead of him. He soon caught up with me. My progress was so slow, every step an act of will. I grasped involuntarily at my tummy while taking a step which reverberated through me. He seemed to notice and glanced towards me. I prickled self-consciously. He would be getting suspicious. Had he also noticed how distracted I was? Would he guess why? I wished that I did not have to walk with him beside me. I felt extraordinarily vulnerable.

The corridor seemed endless, but at last I reached the examination room. With relief I almost fell into the black plastic chair to which Richard had gestured. I did not allow myself to relax, though, lest my face should show the lines of contortion which I felt I must suppress. I was still so afraid of being considered a coward. I wanted to prove that I *would not* lose my composure. I worked for the man: I didn't want to give him a reason to stop respecting me. With hindsight, however, I can see that I was seeking to prove to myself – desperately! – that I could not and would not "fail".

I answered Richard's questions very briefly, almost curtly, for even the effort of speaking increased my discomfort; but I was honest. Having scribbled a few notes, Richard leaned over to take my pulse. There was silence as he counted.

He fiddled with his watch, his face puzzled. It was new: a fancy digital one from one of his lecturing trips abroad. Had he still not worked out how to use it, I wondered? I would normally have teased him – maybe it was too complicated for him – but today there was none of our usual light-hearted banter. I closed my eyes, sensing that I was beginning to take on the passive role of a patient. I felt I was being forced to face up to myself, to "give in". I couldn't overcome the pain either by fighting it or by ignoring it. It was overcoming me.

"136?" The surprise in Richard's voice was mixed with obvious concern. After being so accustomed to fighting for a doctor to take my condition seriously, I now did not quite know what to say. But Richard was not waiting for me to reply; he was counting once again.

"Your pulse is 136, Jane." His face, normally rather mischievous with his dark moustache and huge dimple, was quite neutral. "Bit high, isn't it?" His endeavours to remain unperturbed in front of me were undermined by his pen circling my pulse rate strongly on my case notes. "I'd better examine you."

As I clambered on to the couch, raising my legs slowly to avoid any jerky movement jarring at my abdomen, I realized it was no use pretending any longer. I could have wept – but not just from the pain. My mind was totally confused, not knowing whether to be relieved that at last I was being seen as I really was, or to be afraid of the seriousness of my situation. Physical pain and emotional distress form a potent and destructive partnership.

After he had finished, Richard straightened his arms and leaned the palms of his hands on the couch.

"You know what this means, don't you?" It was more of a statement than a question. I opened my mouth to reply but I couldn't speak. "I'll book theatre for you to be done at 7p.m.," he continued. I looked at the wall-clock: 5p.m. "But I'll make sure the ward is ready to receive you immediately."

He shuffled slightly. He knew me well enough to know that I like people to come straight to the point, instead of waffling around a subject – and he would also know that, given half a chance, I would have questioned and resisted everything.

"Hang on!" I cleared my throat. I could see he was resolute, but my mind swam with questions. "What do you think is happening? Why is this episode so much worse than ever before?"

"Maybe an ectopic. You have all the signs."

I gazed towards the bare gloss-painted wall. So . . . maybe I had been pregnant after all, but the baby was in the Fallopian tube. For some reason, I did not feel sorry for this baby as I did when I nursed other women with ectopics.

Instead, I was full of regret that I hadn't enjoyed all the glee of a first pregnancy.

Matthew would have been delighted, and so proud of me. I would have borne my parents' first grandchild. They would have been thrilled. My mother and I could have enjoyed the unique relationship of a mother and her expectant daughter, and my father would have shared his delight differently. "My darling daughter," he used to call me.

And I had always anticipated relishing every aspect of being pregnant (or as much as was reasonable!), especially once I'd qualified as a midwife. I'd have taken pleasure ensuring that I looked elegant in pretty dresses, relishing this occasion when being a girl was an advantage instead of being "sissy".

These thoughts flashed across my mind within one second. All this had suddenly become impossible.

The implications were far-reaching. The previous June, during another emergency operation, Richard had had to remove one ovary and Fallopian tube. If this was an ectopic pregnancy now, it was in my only remaining Fallopian tube. Once this other side had been removed, as Richard was possibly going to do in two hours, then I would no longer be able to have a baby. I was not only saying goodbye to my first, but to my only possible pregnancy.

I tried not to consider such an idea. "What if it's not an ectopic?" My voice lacked conviction.

"Then I'll have to open you up to see what it *is*." Richard was certainly not going to budge an inch. "I'll see you in theatre," he said firmly.

Back up the corridor, I could not avoid being seen by others on the staff – my friends. Even with the supposed "security" of being taken seriously by Richard, I still could not allow myself to trust anyone else enough to indicate that I was in great pain. Fear continued to taunt me: what if, in two hours, I was found to have nothing much wrong? I would be proved to have been complaining about nothing, and only sissies did that! Rather than risk such a horrifying label, I struggled to hide my apprehension, saying airily, "Oh! I'm off for another operation, folks. Unzipping me again!" And they laughed, as my words suggested they should; but in my heart I was begging for someone to sit down beside me and simply weep with me.

Matthew was quiet as he escorted me to the ward. When faced with a tangle of problems he never speculates as to what might happen. He waits. Thus he did not comment on anything, but he kept me going with his quiet sympathy and love. He was well practised at the whole ritual of my illness, hospitalization and surgery. He had seen me through it five times before.

They were kind enough to me on the ward, though I felt impatient at being subjected to all their questionings. Partly I was bored at recounting the history of my illness yet again, and partly I longed to escape from the intensity of physical suffering. Having to repeat my story gave me less time alone to compose myself and – I suppose – to pray.

"The answer to that question is in my notes," I sighed to a junior nurse at last. She slipped out of my room, biting her lip. Poor girl. A sister was probably a daunting enough prospect for her to nurse, without my putting her in her place like that.

Once I had been prepared for theatre, I valued my short time alone until 7p.m. I wasn't praying in a formal way, just thinking in front of God. I knew he was with me, though now, as so often, I couldn't feel him. I kept placing myself in his hands, asking him to help me to accept how I was. So much putting-on of a brave face in front of others had made it difficult for me to understand exactly how I was, even within myself.

Very soon, it seemed, I was being roused from the anaesthetic. I recognized the sensations from previous operations: the thud as I was lifted from the trolley and dumped back into bed, the inability to cough without pain piercing through me, the helplessness of feeling completely at the mercy of others.

I suddenly became aware of someone beside me.

"Can you hear me, Jane?" It was Richard's voice. I grunted and flickered my eyes but they were too heavy to stay open. "How do you feel?" He was very kind.

"Fine, thanks," I croaked, my usual evasive reply. He would know how I felt; there was no need for me to launch into a moan.

"Well, I, um, thought I'd pop down to see you, to tell you about it."

"What did you find?" Four whole words required a big breath, and I regretted it. Big breaths were very painful.

"It . . . er . . . it wasn't too good, actually." He sounded quite tense, fiddling with coins in his pocket while he spoke. "Sometimes with an acute infection you get fluid accumulating in the Fallopian tubes and sometimes there's a little pus. But Jane, you had lots of pus. And it wasn't neatly contained in your tube. It was all over your pelvis."

I swallowed. This meant that I had acute peritonitis: a serious abdominal infection. There was a pause.

"I knew you'd find it hard to believe, so I tried to take a photo." He knew my hang-ups all right. "Unfortunately the camera wouldn't work: it was broken! You'll just have to take my word for it."

The impact of his words hadn't sunk in yet.

"I stitched you together again without poking around making things worse," he said. "And I've started you on constant intravenous antibiotics for five days." I knew that putting drugs directly into the bloodstream was a much more rigorous way of dealing with infection than the pills which I'd been taking since Wednesday.

For the first time, I began to realize that Richard was treating this – me! – very seriously. He was still hovering beside me. He was quiet, uneasy, solemn. I rarely saw him like this: only occasionally, when he was grieved at seeing a young patient with cancer. He hated being unable to cure people.

"I think I'd better phone Matthew to tell him." He sounded a bit happier now that he'd thought of something positive to do. He paused. "I want you both to know that he can come in and see you any time."

This final comment before he walked slowly away to the telephone was the one which made me sense for myself a little of the seriousness of my condition. In those days, to be allowed to visit someone in hospital at any time was a privilege reserved for relatives of people who were really ill – not for those just recovering from operations, and certainly not for the frauds. I was extremely slow in allowing the facts to percolate through to me, but at last it did begin to dawn on me that I really was very ill.

The trouble was that, so strong was my fear of being labelled a "sissy", I fought against and denied my feelings that I was in pain in order to put on a brave face. I told myself that, however rotten I felt, I must not trust feelings. I pushed to the back of my mind any question that I could in fact be in pain, so effectively that I took a long time to believe it. Richard and, later, Matthew had to repeat over and over to me how I actually was, before I could believe that complaining of pain did not necessarily make me unacceptable.

And once I did begin to believe it, I actually became really excited. It was strange to be elated psychologically when, physically, I was very low. But it seemed a wonderful release to know that others – those who truly *knew* – did not think I had been moaning and moping about nothing. I felt a certain amount of glee and, I suppose, pride, that I had reached a goal I'd set for myself in early childhood – that of being brave, of not allowing pain to "win" over me.

Matthew's visit gave me even more reason to feel vindicated. I was lying very still in the bed when he came, and I was unusually passive. I hardly opened my eyes, nor spoke. He stroked my hand gently.

"Richard phoned me last night, you know," he said steadily.

I nodded: "He said he was going to."

"He said he didn't know how you'd managed to climb the stairs and walk into the department yesterday when you went to see him." I smiled. "He was bewildered. He said, 'If it had been you or me, Matthew, we'd only have got there by being carried in on a stretcher!'"

My chest glowed inside me. I felt just as I used to, many years before, when I had proved to my brothers (or myself) that I could do brave or daring things like climbing the pear tree to the very top. It was all as if I was experiencing, once again, the exhilaration of climbing a different pear tree, and as if my exhilaration were so great that it blinded me to the danger of how those high branches could also swing precariously in the wind.

Matthew continued, "He also told me of his resolve never again to believe your face when you're unwell."

I smiled again, relaxing into feeling understood.

When I opened my eyes I saw his face furrowed as he spoke again. "I'm glad he seems to understand. But . . . " and he held my hand more tightly. He was troubled. "My dear Jane. He's obviously concerned about you. He said you're seriously ill." His voice faltered a little.

I was quiet. "I know," was all I could say.

Time was measured according to the constant drip, drip of my intravenous infusion. Even this high dose of two different antibiotics did not bring the dramatic improvement which everybody had expected. When the course had finished I still remained far from well. The February days stretched into a week, and even a month. March turned to April.

Easter approached and I was still lying in the same bed in hospital. I had only been allowed home once or twice for just a few days at a time. I may have looked the same; but all the time I was becoming weaker.

I became increasingly passive, withdrawing into myself and becoming more difficult to reach. It was not a conscious choice but, I suspect, a way of defending myself. I was afraid, but I didn't know how to say it. I didn't know how to ask for help. Perhaps I hoped, I now suspect, that if anyone *did* truly care, they would see my need and would come and venture into where I was hiding, and comfort me. If that was my subconscious hope, the strategy didn't work, because nobody understood. I didn't understand myself! I didn't give enough clues as to where or how I was.

Whatever the reason, I became distant. I had to be cajoled into eating food. The nurses had to pour my drinks and pass them to me in order to maintain my fluid intake. I had to be encouraged and helped to sit up, because I no longer wanted to prove anything, least of all that I was trying hard to make progress. Certainly I did not muster the energy to hold a book, never mind concentrate on reading it. I simply looked forward to the brief release brought to me by the painkilling drugs, although I loathed the side-effects so much that even *that* respite was tainted by its own dread.

My spirits began to flag. There was no fight left in me. I had lost interest in living: survival with so much pain seemed too daunting. Two or three times I was allowed home for some days, to see if that would help to raise my morale and bring back my normally huge drive to live. Each time, I had to be readmitted within a week or so for painkilling and anti-sickness injections. Medically, there was very little else that could be done for me: I had been pumped full of drugs, vitamins and even sherry, courtesy of the National Health Service! Yet I remained pale, listless, uninterested, ill and in pain. Always I was in pain – more pain, I feared, than I would be able to bear.

During one of my spells out of hospital, I stayed in the home of one of Matthew's college lecturers, Tina. In hospital I had yearned to be nearer to Matthew and I also wanted to be within the deeply caring fellowship of the theological college where Matthew spent each day.

A group of students had met to pray every Monday since I had been admitted to hospital in February. They and others had also reached out to me by visiting me, or by writing to me, or by sending thoughtful messages via Matthew. Their compassion communicated something of God's love, in strong contrast to how isolated I felt in hospital. With persuasion, Richard had conceded that I could be discharged into Tina's care.

Poor Tina: I shudder to think what she had to bear! I was low and debilitated, yet I look back on those few days in her home as an oasis where I was able to drink in comfort and love. I glimpsed something then that was more significant than I realized for years . . . decades. Because there, at Tina's home, I began to feel – though I could not then articulate it – that there is a simplicity of healing. It is often overlooked, I think, especially in a world where technological advance and psychological self-consciousness devour our attention until we become distracted from the direction of real healing. Thus, a patient's pathway may be through pain, but the route towards this simplicity of healing is paved with the most basic attitudes that lie in the hands of every human being. There is a great (but sadly untapped) value in the demonstration of tenderness, care, and – dare one speak openly of this? – yes: love. These go so very far in leading a person towards the simplicity of healing. They make the difference between a life that feels worthless and one that feels worth living. I believe that this simplicity incorporates a wonderful power.

In Tina's flat meantime, Matthew and I could see more clearly how far from my normal self I was, simply because we were nearer to one another. We were both confronted by the extent to which my pain imposed on the expression of our relationship. We did not feel free to enjoy quiet, intimate conversations because the unspoken tension of my illness prevented us from being totally relaxed; of course our usually playful physical expression of our love was completely thwarted.

I began to wonder if Matthew ever considered how much better off he might have been if he had married someone else. I asked him what he would do if I should die. Each time I asked, he talked of returning to Sarawak, where he had once taught. We both knew that he would never be able to fulfil this desire with me, because of my medical history.

The seed of doubt was sown in my mind. Would it not be to Matthew's benefit if I were to die? Of course he would mourn, he would grieve – but would he not ultimately be more free if he were not burdened by me, living in pain?

Throughout my sleepless nights I pondered the burden I thought I was to others. My conclusion was always the same. However hard I tried to make the gift of my life outweigh the burden of it, I failed. I was certain that I was more burden than gift, both to myself and to others.

Even apart from Matthew, I thought of the burden I was on Tina, on others having to visit me. I could not grasp that they themselves might be gaining anything. I saw weakness as a waste – particularly my own. I did not recognize any value in my life, either for myself or for those close to me. I had struggled on for so long, that eventually I became weary and sick of life itself. Finally one day, I gave up hope.

It all happened following a telephone call to the hospital, seeking help. I felt desperate for Richard to understand that I was unable to tolerate the dreadful pain any longer.

I was unable to speak to Richard himself, but another sister, Pat, listened very understandingly. She took my message and promised to phone me back.

I sat on the floor, waiting, hoping. I was still hoping, then: surely *something* could help me?

The silence in Tina's flat was suddenly broken by Pat's return phone call.

"Jane?" Pat spoke very gently.

"Yes, hi." Ridiculously I covered my desperation by adopting a jovial voice. "What did Richard say?"

"He said, 'Keep going.'"

My heart sank. This was *not possible*!

"But Pat, I phoned because I've run out of resources to be able to."

"Well, he said that when or if things get back to being as bad as they were in February, then you must come back to him."

How could I explain myself more clearly? "Pat, things *are* back to being as they were in February. In fact I feel worse. I've no strength left with which to fight now."

"You're that bad, Jane?" Pat wanted to be sure she had the message right. "Remember how seriously ill you were then."

I remembered all right. "Pat, this is urgent. I can't go on."

"Hang on. I'll phone you back again."

I knew that, each time she went, she must be interrupting Richard in between patients at his busy Wednesday morning clinic. Normally I would have been helping him. I knew he hated interruptions. I shuddered with apprehension.

I knelt on the floor of Tina's hallway, leaning over the low table while I waited the second time. I could not face the tedium of struggling to a comfortable chair. No chair was comfortable in any case – no chair, nor bed, nor any position. I could not escape.

Pat did not take long. This time her voice, though still gentle, was strained. "I've spoken again to Richard and explained more clearly how you are." She hesitated. "He said that you must be assured you can come into hospital at any time, day or night, for adequate pain relief."

I could not believe my ears. I was being given the instructions we give to patients having terminal care. This was what we said to patients when we could not cure them . . .

I was careful to hide any emotion from my voice when I replied. "Was there nothing else he said?" I asked. "Can't he do anything, Pat?"

Pat was obviously choosing her words carefully. "He said there is nothing more positive he can do." Then she added, "He felt very helpless and very sorry for you."

I replaced the receiver. So, that was it then. Clumsily, I made my way to the sitting-room. My mind was completely vacant, numb, except for the words, repeatedly, ". . . nothing more . . . he can do . . . nothing more . . ."

I do not recall how many people I stared through as that day progressed. It was as if I had been given an anaesthetic that numbed me without giving me the release of sleep.

One visit I do remember, though. Matthew was with me when Colin, the college principal, came. I thought of him as a shy man with little time for small talk in his busy life, but he had been wonderful throughout my illness, visiting me frequently in hospital. I was very grateful, though I stood enough in awe of him to fear that, if I were to share my deepest reactions, he might find them rather trite.

Colin asked me how I felt. My answer was, I thought, suitably objective. I avoided telling him how I felt emotionally and chose instead to give him factual information. I reported my phone call that morning.

Colin sat for a long time, keeping his gaze on me until at last he asked, "Does this mean death, Jane?"

I was startled.

"Pardon?" I asked, killing time. I was dreadfully uncomfortable. I was not used to talking intimately with Colin and he was pretty near the bone now. I was terrified I might cry – courageous me, in front of Colin to whom I did not wish to appear a weepy woman! And anyway, what would Matthew think? I was acutely embarrassed that he was there, listening, because we hadn't faced this question together. How did Colin dare to be so direct as this?

He repeated his question. "Does this mean death?"

I knew he expected an answer from me. I looked at Matthew and I saw, with some relief, that he was not surprised by Colin. I tried to follow his example and keep calm.

"I suppose it could . . . yes."

I will never forget Colin's help, though I cannot recall any specific words he said. I just know he stayed with us. He counselled us, prayed with us. With his help, Matthew and I joined hands and faced the possibility of my death, together. We had not been left alone.

But that afternoon, something snapped. Thoughts of release became urgent. Suddenly I felt unable to wait any longer to be taken to heaven. I could not bear, any more, to live here.

This was my Gethsemane. The pain was too much. God was asking too much of me. I had that huge bottle of pills which Richard had prescribed in February with his "joke" about not taking them all at once. Wouldn't it help me, and Matthew, and Tina and Colin, and all those in college, if I just speeded things up? Wouldn't that give a nice happy ending instead of my having to bear this seemingly endless pain and confusion?

In the middle of that night the temptation became unbearable.

"Tina!" I cried out loud from my bedroom.

And to God I cried in a whisper, "Let this cup pass from me . . . "

CHAPTER TWO

"NOT AS I WILL, BUT AS YOU WILL"

Matthew 26:39b

If Tina had preached to me about the goodness of God, I would never have come through as I did. The fact was, God seemed not to care a toss that I was at the end of my tether. Yet even in the depths of that desperate anguish, there was in me some stirring of affirmation that I wanted what God wanted, and that meant that I must not take my own way out.

"I mustn't, must I?" I whispered, clutching the bottle of pills.

Tina's curlers clung resolutely to the ends of her hair. Acutely embarrassed, I watched her eyes take in the scene, her ample bosom heaving somewhat breathlessly with anxiety. I had set a bucket beside my bed, lest an overdose should make me vomit; a towel, laid neatly across the sheet, lest I should make a mess; but most obvious of all must have been the loss of hope on my face.

Quickly she moved forward to kneel beside the bed, taking both my hands in hers. "Have you taken any?" Her voice was earnest: she had realized immediately the implications of what she saw.

I shook my head.

40

I could not speak now. Words seemed trite, inadequate, too shallow to describe the depths I felt. It was as if my experience of suffering had led me to see over the edge of a cliff where, far below, lay a whole world.

As Tina knelt beside me, a silent bond between us began to infuse warmth into my numbness against life. If I felt nothing else, I was at least glad somebody had come to me; somebody was holding me while I looked into that abyss. I suspect that she, too, saw the same picture as I.

Eventually I spoke. "God is asking too much of me."

The last thing I wanted was theology or anything – anything – other than loving understanding. I needed to hear that, yes, this really was unbearable, and indeed that the worst, most devastating aspect was that God was not rescuing me from intolerable pain.

The compassion in Tina's eyes did not fade. With relief, I realized that she was not judging me. It was as if she knew that we were both looking at the infinite, the unanswerable. To have imagined we could give an answer with our finite minds would have been to deny what we were seeing.

With Tina's ability to hold my anguish without denying it or explaining it away, came the softness of tears. They began to flow down the cheeks of us both: tears of agony but also of relief that I was not being condemned for hurling such strong questions into the air.

"How can he allow this pain to go on so long when he's *able* to take it away? How can I express to him that this is too much . . . ?" I was crying aloud now.

Slowly, very gently, Tina began to speak. Her voice was very soft, almost a whisper. "I don't know," she said when my sobbing began to ease. She knew I was not asking for answers: I was shouting at God. I was trying to demand that he explain himself to me.

Tina must have known that she would have squashed me if she had sounded strong in the face of my weakness.

She must have been aware that we were both at the mercy of God and where he would lead us. She showed no pride that she had not been tempted as I had been only minutes before. She knew that she could have been led to the same place as me, had God so allowed.

"I don't understand him," she said softly. "He does seem to ask an awful lot of some people sometimes." She looked at her hands, and her voice trailed away. I began to sense that she herself had suffered a time when God had seemed harsh to her.

There was a silence between us: a silence that warmed me because I felt that the emotional and spiritual pain was shared, and that meant mine was *share-able* . . . and one of my fears was that I was cut off, isolated and alone with my anguish. Here I was feeling understood – and however much or little didn't really matter. *Any* help was help.

I could see that Tina herself was struggling, not just with my distress but also, I sensed, with a memory of her own. And here I could see something else: that although I felt that all my pain and distress was only useless and fruitless and even something for me to feel ashamed of, I knew that her gentleness could only have arisen from pain of some sort in her own experience. Thus, her experience had not been fruitless: I felt embraced by the very fruit of what she had borne. I remember thinking that Tina's voice was so full of gentleness and so free of judgement, she must surely have come to accept whatever had been her pain. She had not resigned herself to what had happened: she had accepted it. And that is not one step but a whole journey: one that I was to discover many, many years later.

What a path that is, leading from resignation to acceptance; I have found it to be unwalkable except with the Lord as my Shepherd.

As Tina's love and empathy infused into me – almost as if her arms were holding me to this earth – I began to feel safe enough to relax a little. Thus, instead of fighting against everything, I began to accept at least *something*. I – the fighter by nature – began to see that the strength God gives may be strength to *embrace* what happens – even when it is hard – and not always to fight *against* it.

I lay back against the pillows for the first time that night. Slowly the tension began to ease just a little while Tina's compassion shone through her words. As she gradually unfolded her story, I realized that she was not surprised by my being at the end of my tether. She had been in that place herself. She was able to share the burden of my pain because she recognized it. It was good for me to be taken into the heart of someone else's suffering. This was true compassion – "suffering with": because she had refused to run away from the hard questions within herself, determining instead to face them, so she could also face them in me.

It was not her story itself that I found so moving, but the manner in which she talked. Her quietness and calmness spoke, more clearly than any words, of her complete acceptance of me in my despair. She was offering me the same acceptance that she had found for herself. She had a peace that softened the harshness of the fact that she knew she would never completely understand God's wisdom. She had therefore allowed some questions to remain. She accepted the mystery of suffering. The more I listened, the more encouraged I felt. Not that I was pleased that she had suffered so much, though possibly there was some comfort in knowing I was not alone in sharing, even in a tiny way, how Jesus maybe felt in Gethsemane on the night *he* felt he could take no more. But the real source of my encouragement was the sheer relief that I was not being judged as being dreadfully unchristian for feeling as I did. Knowing that Tina had been taken to similar depths and desperation – and her story caused me to admire her rather than despise her – maybe I could dare to stop condemning myself and also shed my awful sense of shame.

I suddenly realized that many people suffer like this, but that they do not dare to talk about it for fear that such an intimately personal experience might be explained away glibly by someone who simply cannot understand.

Before leaving me to rest for the last few hours of the night, Tina prayed with me. In fact, "prayer" almost sounds too heavy a word: there was nothing heavy or pious-sounding, and I did not feel imposed upon. She spoke slowly, even haltingly, respecting the very vulnerable place in my heart that I had invited her to share.

In quietness and stillness, Tina sought God's will with me. She asked that if, as it seemed, God was not going to rescue me from the suffering, I might know him in it. Her prayer could not have been more appropriate. This was one of the times in life when pleading with God to let me escape would have meant that I would lose touch with God. If I was to accept life – which is his command – I needed to accept the struggle. That pathway was the route to finding his presence, that loving presence which never leaves us nor forsakes us even in the harsh reality of pain.

The following day dawned bright and sunny. Everything seemed to have a heightened significance; every aspect of the world going round drew my attention. The sky was clear and blue, the spring air fresh. While I waited for Matthew to call in on his way to morning worship, I was intrigued to watch the birds in the trees outside. They were not fighting their way through life. They just got on with it, busily content with everyday things. They chirped and sang; they flitted across to a different branch for a change of scene; they looked for worms on the lawn; they flew high and swooped down again. They were carefree. They were not questioning how long they would live. When difficulties arose they would either overcome them or they would die. They were not overburdened about that.

Perhaps, I thought, I could learn from the birds.

My musings were interrupted by the welcome click of the door. The moment Matthew entered I put my arms right round him in a tight hug. In holding him as I did, I think I was acknowledging a deeply subconscious intent to hold on to life in this world.

Gradually I dared to give him hints as to what had happened during the night. The more he listened, the more I felt freed to speak. Oh, the relief that he accepted what I said without condemning me! He skipped his first lecture in order to prolong our blessed time together, silently affirming our allegiance to one another. The reassurance I felt from him – and later from others – was a lifeline. I was pretty astonished that I *could* be comforted: I had written off any expectation of that altogether when I had given up hope.

And so that comfort brought courage: the courage to be weak. Strengthened by that, I experienced some sort of breakthrough. I began to grow deeper and deeper into an acceptance of God's will for me, however hard it was to be . . . and this occasion was strong enough for me to be able to revisit the dark edge of the abyss in later years.

Other people noticed and remarked upon the deepdown spirit of peace that welled up from within me, but I was still critically ill. My week in Tina's home drew to an end as the Easter holiday approached. I very much wanted to go to the final Thursday evening communion. I wanted to be in college among so very many caring Christians who had supported me in prayer through the long months.

It was a struggle to go the few yards from Tina's college flat to the chapel, but I wanted to make the effort. I remember Caroline helping to dress me, as I felt too weak for even that exertion. Once outside, I leaned my weak body against a supportive arm. Almost every step was an act of will:

Just get yourself to that handrail. Walk! Keep going!

Rest your weight on that door-handle for a minute, then

walk again. Get to the next door before stopping again. Force yourself! Don't lose your momentum.

I recall one door being opened for me by someone who had heard how ill I was but who had not seen me since February. As I walked through the door, his face suddenly froze. He almost saluted, jumping to attention with a click of his heels. I wanted to speak the words that were in my head: Don't worry, I'm not in my coffin yet!

The chapel doors were open when I approached, and I could hear the hum of conversation before the service began. It was two months since I had been part of a service, and my spirits rose excitedly. Although it was only 48 hours since that terrible night with Tina, now, as I neared the chapel, I knew for myself that God had given me a new peace. Assuredly, this peace passes all human understanding – because, humanly speaking, nothing had changed. I had no reason to be peaceful, no new hope of cure or of the release of death being any nearer, no magic pills to relieve the pain and nausea. Yet I was filled right up to the top with God's peace.

I was handed my hymn-book by a student named John. I felt as if my very soul were being filled even more with God's peace: so much that there was also an absurd joyfulness in my heart, and the radiance of this joy merged into an enormous love towards everyone. I almost fear writing this lest it sound ridiculous, and yet it is true, and perhaps this is what every Christian is given when the time comes for them to be drawn closer to God, in death but also – as I experienced at college there – in life, here, on earth! This can only have been a heavenly gift. It was as if I was darting from one corner of my heart to another, discovering new and wonderful presents from my Lord at every turn.

John was the first person whom I greeted as I became aware of what the Lord had given me. Taking the book from his outstretched hand, I could see he was looking at me closely. I beamed at him and even then I remember thinking that the broadest of smiles could not reflect the joy within me.

Years later, I learned that John ran straight home after the service had begun and told his wife excitedly, "I've seen Jane Grayshon – can't you come and see her too? It's her face . . . " He was quite breathless from running. "Although she was stooping physically, her face glowed! She was absolutely radiant." His wife couldn't come, but John returned to his sidesman's duties. Later that evening he was inspired to write a beautiful poem that he gave me years afterwards, when he told me his side of what had happened that evening.

This was not a passive submission to what I could not change. I had not resigned myself to God's will. I had done something much more positive than that. I had begun to embrace God's will: "Not as I will, but as you will, O Lord." As a result I discovered that some precious fruit was growing even within my suffering – was it despite it, or because of it, I ask now? Certainly it grew from the very root of acceptance which Tina had offered to me.

The following two months were a hard test of this acceptance. Nothing changed dramatically. It was as if the whole scenario was held still, as if God was holding the whole situation before me and asking, "Will you still accept my will, Jane? Or are you merely accepting my will because you hope that will bring about a change in the situation? For how long will you endure for my sake? As long as I desire, or until you run out of patience?"

But that gift that God had given me increased my trust in him. Indeed, as the weeks of April passed into May, so my acceptance of his will grew.

During this lull in the storm, while I became no better, but no worse either, someone from the prayer group heard me comment that only the sunshine in the Bahamas would do me any good. A seed was sown in her mind.

There were about ten couples who had committed themselves to prayer each week, all students on meagre grants. Yet their desire was to be open to what God wanted. They were willing to do anything practical to help Matthew and me – not "just" to pray.

Within a week of my comment, I was presented with an envelope. I could see that it was a card – another one among many, all assuring me that friends cared about me and were thinking of me. I laid this one on the table beside my bed. I would enjoy Caroline's visit now and could look forward to opening it later after she had gone.

"Aren't you going to open it then?" Caroline's voice almost sounded hurt, but her eyes sparkled with excitement.

"Oh . . . all right then," I conceded. Wearily, I slit open the white envelope and pulled out the card.

Something slipped out from between the folds on to my blanket, followed by a ten-pound note. I handled the money and then picked up the other paper from between the folds. It was a cheque. I turned it over to read it: "Four hundred and ten pounds only".

I looked at the words incredulously. Caroline was almost dancing on the bed. She knew the wonderful freedom and pleasure of giving in response to God. She, and the whole group, had not held fund-raising events. They had prayed to God to help me; they had listened to him; now they responded by giving whatever they felt right. They had managed to double a gift Matthew's mother had lovingly promised to us.

"You can have your holiday in the sun!" said Caroline, impatient with my stunned silence. Her voice was almost squeaking, such was her joy in giving.

I had only just begun to believe what we had been given,

when Colin dropped by once again. About twice each day, he showed his continuing care and support.

I handed him the envelope.

He was kneeling on the floor beside my bed, just as Tina had done only three nights before. Now it was his turn to be silenced. His eyes moistened as he witnessed such love and involvement of Christian friends.

When others heard of the cheque they too joined in with their prayerful contributions until we could have a really big holiday. "If all you can do is lie down, then go and do that – but in the sun," they said.

So we did. After browsing through brochures, we took off. We had chosen a tiny island 50 miles from Madeira, with only one hotel and a long white beach. This was the longest spell I had out of hospital in the midst of what otherwise seemed an imprisonment between February and July. For ten days we felt free – free from hospital routines, visiting hours, telephone calls from caring relations. For those precious days, we were blessed by one another, together and alone.

Matthew's biggest problem now was stopping me from swimming! My natural love of water and sport, combined with the lure of the balmy turquoise water, almost overcame common sense. I lacked the physical strength to swim safely, so I had to be content with quick dips to cool off from the sun. Instead, I developed a beautiful suntan.

Unfortunately my honey-coloured skin, which made me look so well, was misleading. My temporary respite was not to last long after our return.

I accompanied Matthew to college at the beginning of the new term. Our welcome back was wonderful. Some people felt as if I had returned from the dead – the last time they had seen me was at the communion service before the Easter holiday, when I had been so very ill.

"Jane – you look so much better! You look wonderful."

Some people were more misled. "You are so much better," they said. Perhaps neither they nor I realized how much my colour, heightened by the sun, belied the condition of my inside.

"You still look radiant, Jane, but how are you really?" That sort of comment came from those who took slightly more time to enquire how I felt, rather than presuming that my appearance represented how I felt.

Those who knew that I enjoyed a good leg-pull grinned. "Trust you to wear a white blouse just to accentuate your tan!" I twinkled in reply. Yes, I had to admit I did enjoy being the envy of so many people!

I was wearing a white blouse again not many days later, when our latent hopes for a gradual convalescence suddenly plummeted.

It was during another Thursday evening communion service in the college chapel that I realized my abdominal pain was much worse. When pain is severe, it is often hard to say that it is slightly better or slightly worse: pain is always bad! But this Thursday evening there was no doubt that it was growing very much worse.

I resisted my first temptation to whisper to Matthew. I did not think that I could get out of chapel, if he suggested that we leave. Instead, I held on to a hope that it was a spasm that would pass. I heard nothing of the service. My thoughts were entirely taken up with plans as to how I could get out of chapel without drawing attention to myself.

The door was not too far away. But panic rose in me as I glanced towards it and saw the row filled with people whom I would need to pass on my way out. They were all men, too. I speculated: They're sure to think I'm a sissy for going out. So I can't go.

Graham, Matthew's tutor, who had remained so close to us throughout my illness, was just on Matthew's right. I knew that I would be unable to walk upright: I'm supposed to be better. Graham might suppose I'm trying to attract attention to myself, if I walk out bent double now.

I was paralyzed by my old, deep-seated fears. Graham had been so very caring towards us, I did not want to lead him to think I was fussing.

This time, though, the physical pain became more acute than my fears. Waiting for it to pass did not work. It got worse until I reached a level of pain that I had not previously known to exist.

A hymn began. I prodded Matthew.

"Can't get up," I garbled. Once again, every word cost me extra breath; every breath meant more pain searing through me.

"Well, just sit through the hymn, silly," Matthew replied vaguely, without looking at me.

I am normally very pleased when Matthew can enjoy times of release from being weighed down by the solemnity of my suffering. However, this was one occasion when there was no doubt that I had to shatter his freedom and make him realize what I meant.

I slipped my hand into his, ready to try to explain. Taking my hand, Matthew was shocked to feel the icy clamminess: it was positively slippery with cold perspiration. He looked at me, then, seeing my face for the first time, whispered, "Oh, my dear Jane!"

The piano introduction was over and everyone else stood up to sing. I was thankful for the element of privacy that that brought, for now I could be seen by only one row of people between me and the door.

"Come on." Matthew left no room for discussion as to whether or not I should leave the service.

"Can't get up."

I began to be distressed by my helplessness.

Matthew almost lifted me and continued to take much of

my weight very discreetly as he accompanied me towards the vestry door. Most of the men were immersed in their singing, but as I passed Graham, I was again tormented by the fear that "weak" meant unacceptable. So, despite the terrible pain, despite my need to concentrate on every move towards the door, somehow I mustered a big smile for him. It was such a bluff, aimed at preventing him from having any suspicion of what was going on.

The effect of that smile was twofold. First, it protected me in my embarrassment at being so vulnerable – I did not know how to cope with being visibly outfaced by pain. But of course, while my smile may have been successful in avoiding "making a fuss", it also had the effect of cutting Graham off from the opportunity to offer care or help. It was a high price for me to pay: what I wanted most was – and is – to feel others' care. They cannot cure the pain, but they can comfort me within it. And, whether I liked it or not, I needed help. Yet I did not allow myself to receive it.

Once the chapel door was shut behind me, Matthew looked for a chair. There was none there. I leaned forwards over the table with my arms outstretched, and I laid my head on my hands. This felt the only thing I could do to find any relief at all; yet I knew I could not stay there.

"What shall we do?" he asked.

"Must tell Richard." He was the only one who could really do anything to help. I knew something had happened inside me about which he must be told. Even though it was evening, there was no doubt that he must see me immediately.

I raised myself again, catching sight of my reflection in the wall mirror as I did so. With some horror I saw that my suntan had been replaced by ashen white.

I had to move on. Leaning heavily on Matthew, I staggered to the staircase. For the first time I could sit down, on one of the steps.

"What do you want me to do?" Matthew repeated; but this time I think he knew that I was beyond being able to think rationally, as he could.

"Can't move," was all I could say in a staccato voice. I nearly panicked at finding myself so helplessly paralyzed by pain. "I simply can't."

And yet, strange as it may seem, amid this entire trauma, I was still aware of a deep peace and acceptance undergirding me.

I sat rigid on the step.

Matthew gave me an ultimatum. "You either let me phone Richard, or the doctor, or I get an ambulance," he stated firmly.

I couldn't contemplate an ambulance coming for me while I was conscious! Matthew's ultimatum caused me to muster all my strength again. Slowly, carefully, I pulled myself up and managed to descend a few stairs. Matthew did not press me for an answer – though he must have wondered what on earth would happen next.

By the time I had reached the bottom of the stairs I had agreed to one of his suggestions. We would seek help from the caring home of the college principal and his wife Di.

I could trust Di: trust her not to judge me. She would simply care. As our short spurts of progress brought us towards Di's house, I had some carrot of hope for help.

Di did not disappoint me. Her welcome did not reflect the fact that she and her daughters had been in the middle of their meal when we rang the bell. It was as if she had been expecting us. "Jane!" She held her arm out to me in a quiet, helping gesture. "You're coming in to lie down?" She looked to Matthew for confirmation.

Hands helped me to a comfortable chair. The kind smiles and caring eyes merged into a spinning haze of pain. I began to shiver and shake uncontrollably. Blankets were fetched and wrapped around me.

"What a granny I must look like!" I spluttered, utterly embarrassed even through that dreadful daze. Di started sponging my face and neck with soothing warm water; my hands were submerged and the water was gently swished over them. Allowing them to float eased away some of the shock. The water itself was a therapy; the tender care with which it was done was even more so.

From behind my closed eyes I heard Matthew telephoning from the hall. He was having difficulty getting help. Our family doctor said she could not leave her clinic. Richard was on the golf course and, though his wife had offered to send a message to him, it would be some time before he could do anything.

Matthew returned. He and Di discussed plans. Di ran off to get another doctor, Cathy, whom they knew was in the chapel. Immediate help was needed until Richard could be contacted.

Cathy, though whisked out from the chapel service, was unflustered. She did not persist unnecessarily with her examination of me. She soon assessed what injection I needed, and drove off promptly to fetch it.

The morphine had begun to work by the time Colin returned home. He had not seen the various exits from the chapel service earlier, nor did he know the story behind them. He leapt two at a time up the steps into his house as usual, and paced straight into the room.

He soon switched his quick mind. "You not feeling so good, Jane?" He perched himself on a chair. He would always make time to listen when there was a real need.

"Not wonderful," was my reply. "Silly, isn't it?", and I tried to chuckle lightly, deflecting yet again from the heaviness which I felt.

Someone else gave him details of the hunt for medical assistance, while my mind drifted in a morphine blur. Colin took it all in. He stayed with us for the remainder of the evening, suspending whatever else he had planned to do. Both Matthew and I appreciated the sacrifice of his time – especially because we knew how immensely busy he was. Yet he stopped for those precious hours, simply to be with us.

He was not even "helping" us formally by counselling us. But when visitors dropped in to see me on their way home from college, Colin thoughtfully steered the conversation away from me, recognizing that all I could do was to lie limply on the sofa and allow any conversation to drift over me.

The visitors left, the girls retired upstairs to bed, and only Colin and Di sat on with Matthew and me into the late May twilight.

Tension mounted as the minutes ticked by and still we waited for at least a message from Richard. If we did not hear soon, the effect of the injection would diminish and my state of shock might worsen. Cathy had insisted she would return within two hours to attend to me if I was still not in hospital, but I loathed troubling her. I felt a thorough nuisance and wished I could pull myself together. Once again, it was as if I heard a whispered accusation that I was too cowardly to try hard enough.

Our speculations were stalled by a visit from Graham, Matthew's tutor. He had only just heard where I was and why.

"Why on earth didn't you get Matthew to fetch me out of the chapel?" he asked, half chuckling at my refusal ever to give in, half hurt (I suspect) that I had seemed not to trust him. "We could have carried you down the stairs together."

I curled up at the notion. "Please, don't be hurt," I pleaded.

As usual, Graham discerned the most important issue.

"Are you afraid, Jane?"

I paused before answering. His questions were always worth thinking about.

"I'm so completely taken up in coping with the present, I'm not looking ahead." With the help of the morphine my sentences could be less brief, my words less staccato.

"But now that I'm asking you?" he pursued.

My thoughts raced on to what would be decided about me during the coming night, inevitably in hospital.

"I suppose I am . . . But I'm all right."

Graham knew of my experience of deep inner peace, arising out of the acceptance that even this pain might be under God's hand. He dared to dig deeper with his questions. "What do you fear most of all?"

I let my mind consider for a moment the various possibilities that lay ahead for me, wondering what I feared the most among them. Certainly it was not the possibility of dying which made me fearful: that would have brought so much relief from the pain that it was a welcome idea. That was the clue to my worst fear.

"Continuation of pain with no prospect of relief," I said, numbly. "I fear another anaesthetic, as you know – especially with the memory of not being fully asleep last year before they started doing things to me."

I shuddered as I remembered the tubes being put down my throat, my body being handled as if I was not conscious, and the horror of being unable to move or show any sign that I was still awake.

"And I fear the weakness and the long, long uphill struggle of recovering from a big operation. But those would be just about bearable if they were successful and worthwhile." I paused to think about types of pain, such as labour pain which, though intense and dreadful at the time, is normally forgotten as soon as it brings forth its purpose – a healthy baby. But this was in stark contrast to my current suffering.

"It's the thought of pain with no end, no purpose, no fruit, which is so difficult." Even as I said it I knew that

Graham was helping me, because his questions were so challenging. Had these things remained unspoken, I think I would have remained locked in the fear. Often, disregarding inner fears or trying to keep them covered merely offers them scope for destruction. To bring them out into the open is to bring them to the light of God and to break any power that darkness may have.

Graham understood my answer.

"God doesn't make any mistakes, Jane." How often he had reinforced that truth to me.

I shook my head. "I don't feel this is his mistake." Talking was giving me more confidence in God's will.

Graham smiled. "How are you so sure of that?"

"Because God is in it." I myself was amazed to find that that deep-down tranquillity which I had first experienced back in April had spread from my soul to my mind. Even this immense pain did not quench it. "It's accompanied by such peace, such an assurance of him with me, that I know it's not his mistake." Whatever was to follow that night, I knew I was in God's hands. "I just wish I could get comfortable now."

And Graham, in his wisdom, was able to accept what I was expressing. There is a difference between the theory of accepting God's will even when he does not promise to give us a comfortable life, and the hard grind of enduring suffering when it actually comes.

Alone again with Colin and Di, a quietness settled in the room, although the warm homeliness belied the unspoken tension. We were all awaiting the telephone's ring with increasing urgency. Outside, darkness was falling quickly now and there was a chill in the air. Di tucked the blankets around me again and lit the small lamps on the shelf. As she bent down, soft shadows were cast across her cheeks. It was then that I noticed the anxiety in her face.

Suddenly everyone was jerked away from apprehensive

speculation. For an uncertain moment, Matthew looked quickly to his host, then he strode across to answer the shrill telephone himself.

However many times I had rehearsed Richard's reaction in my mind, however long the hours of waiting had been, I was still surprised to hear the stark reality of the words.

Matthew leaned round the door, relaying Richard's instructions through from the hall into the room. "We're meeting Richard at the hospital in fifteen minutes." That was a statement – no question – and it startled me. "Now, will you manage to go in our car, or should he send an ambulance?"

"Oh, car, please." At least Matthew would be sensitive to drive gently and avoid potholes in the road. "Do I really have to go, though?"

Matthew smiled, withdrew to the phone and let the door close behind him. Colin rose to find my coat; Di came towards me to help me to get up from the sofa. My question warranted no reply.

Somehow, I managed to stand up, but however much I tried, I could not straighten myself completely. I felt humiliated to be so stooped and bent. I had no idea that I was the only one who expected the impossible of myself.

Inch by inch I staggered across that room, wondering at each step how I could cross the few feet to the door. Colin's face was very compassionate: I remember that detail because it was a surprise for me, even a source of confusion. Kindness, instead of mockery, when here I was, so visibly not succeeding in "climbing a pear tree"? He opened the door for me, allowing me to see the slight ramp I had to negotiate to get into the car. At that moment I almost felt too daunted. My dismay must have registered on my face.

"Would it not be best if we lifted you?" Colin asked.

I shook my head. "I'm OK," I muttered. I swallowed

hard and gripped the low garden wall. Matthew hovered beside me.

The ramp loomed ahead of me and I had to reach the top of it as if it had been the pear tree itself. I willed myself: Shuffle one foot forward. You must do it. Take a breath. Now the other foot. Don't crack now . . .

Matthew closed the car door and started the engine. Colin and Di were silhouetted in their doorway against the glowing lights of their warm home. Then, as the car turned, the headlights swished round to illuminate their faces. They smiled and waved. Their hearts were with us.

I clenched my hands as the car moved forwards at last. Still the two figures remained on the threshold, gazing out into our darkness. They waited and watched after us until we were right out of sight. Even when we could no longer see them, we knew that in spirit they were with us, driving into the night.

Their lingering presence was a significant sign of what I was slow to appreciate: that while I suffered, they suffered with me.

CHAPTER THREE

"IF ONE SUFFERS, ALL SUFFER"

1 Corinthians 12:26

It was hard for Matthew to turn from my bedside and leave the hospital: he felt as if he were turning his back on me . . . betraying me, even, in my hour of need. In fact, his "task" of walking away from someone he loved, carrying the particular anguish of one who can only watch helplessly, was probably harder than my task of bearing the visible, physical pain. He, the strong one, had to feel that terrible impotence that there was nothing he could do: only watch, and wait. That was his "suffering".

As he drove homewards down the familiar Nottingham roads, his mind turned over the various scenes in an attempt to come to terms with all that had happened. He was unable to rid himself of the anxiety that arose every time he saw, again, the picture of my pale face. And yet, he reasoned with himself, was this night any different? For so many months he had endured, living beside me on that knife-edge, hovering between serious illness and critical. It had all gone on for so long that we had gradually come to accept it as part of both our lives. Now Matthew was no longer living alongside me with my pain: he was living in his own pain.

And there was also Richard's face, solemn and unmoving. What had been in his mind, Matthew wondered? Was there more he might do to help? Was there further treatment to which he could resort?

Richard had shown no sign of emotion. He had gone through everything in a businesslike manner. He could not show distress lest that should affect his clinical judgement. I was the patient, he the helper. He would surely be failing if he became a victim to suffering as well.

"I'm very sorry," he had said numbly. "Just to complicate matters, I'm afraid that tomorrow I'm off to France for the weekend." His eyes fixed thoughtfully on the shiny hospital floor.

A weekend? That seemed an unbearably long time! I would surely not be able to cling to life until Monday?

Fear must have registered in my eyes, and Richard must have reached the same conclusion. "I must get the professor's opinion," he had announced, walking purposefully to the telephone.

Suddenly, things began to move. After weeks and months of not knowing what to do, the medical profession seemed galvanized into action. I was transferred temporarily to the care of the professor. On the following day, another surgeon was brought in to give his opinion. Richard telephoned from France to hear what was happening.

The major question was whether or not they should operate. They hesitated to do so: I might not survive the anaesthetic. But the professor's reluctance was for a different reason. He was increasingly insistent that they could not be certain what exactly more surgery would hope to achieve.

Once again I was pumped full of injections – a constant infusion of antibiotics, vitamins, nourishment. Whenever Matthew saw me I was lying pale, listless and exhausted by pain.

Then one day everything came to a head. The doctors

held a case conference in the ward. The dynamics had become strained. Richard, back from his holiday weekend, was technically back to being in charge of me: I was "his" patient. However he was junior to the professor. He was surprised that another laparotomy had not been done in his absence, but how could he express this horror to his boss? His judgement was based more on how ill he sensed I was, than on specific medical tests. He was very concerned. In comparison, the professor seemed intent on appearing relaxed about my condition. He had reinforced that impression most firmly by strolling into the ward office for the case conference a whole 40 minutes late.

By now Richard was seething. This time, his suffering was easier to identify and to comprehend. He not only had to endure feeling impotent because he couldn't "make" me better, but also, self-doubt may have crept in because of the dynamics between him and the professor. He therefore barely raised his eyes to greet the latecomer. And none of us guessed then that even the professor could have been feeling pain from the whole situation, that his difficult attitude might have been a tell-tale sign of his own uneasiness. Certainly his opening words did not seem the best way to begin a discussion.

"You've resorted to surgical intervention unnecessarily in the past," came the stinging accusation. Matthew and I were grateful that we were separated from this discussion by a short distance between my bed and the ward office, even though the open door meant that we could hear every word, and could see them through the glass partition.

There was a pause. Richard refused to rise to such bait. Silence was probably the loudest reply he could have given.

The professor flicked through my case notes. "Look at this histology report. 'Normal tissue' is what you removed last time . . . " He thrust the brown folder into Richard's hands.

Richard received it, still in silence. The tension rose: his very competence was being called into question. The expression on his face was ominously dark.

"I am telling you," he replied at last, struggling to steady his voice. "I saw what I removed and I can still see it now. This piece of paper reports what the histology department saw under the microscope. It does not report what was visible to the eye: what *I* saw with my own two eyes."

I sensed that this was almost becoming a jousting session; one could have been forgiven for wondering if they would fight to the kill. "The ovary I removed was macroscopically *ab*normal. It was obviously the cause of Jane's severe abdominal pain. As evidence, she was much improved for six months post operation, until this acute peritonitis flared up again in February."

There was more discussion, until Matthew and I, waiting apprehensively, heard the handle of the office door being rattled somewhat angrily as the door was flung fully open.

Only their heavy footsteps punctuated the strained silence between the two surgeons as they approached my bed. Each man's face appeared firm and hard. Matthew's hand closed more tightly round my thin wrist. He was tense too, waiting to hear what would be the outcome of this "conference".

Richard, though uncharacteristically subdued, nodded kindly to Matthew. It was the professor who, accustomed to acting as chairman, gave their report. "As you know, Jane has had a lot of problems with peritoneal inflammation." He was addressing Matthew rather than me. "She seems to be having continued pain despite our conservative medical treatment on drugs . . . "

"Conservative?!" questioned Richard from the opposite side of the bed, in a whisper which was nevertheless an interruption. He ran his eyes up and down the length of the intravenous infusions with the two lots of strong-dose antibiotics.

"And therefore," the first voice continued more loudly,

"we have decided that there is no course of action left to us except further surgery."

Matthew was uncomfortable at having to receive this information so passively, and especially in this atmosphere. The only active thing he could do was to speak.

"What do you propose?"

My heart beat faster, harder.

The professor hesitated slightly before meeting Matthew's uncertain gaze.

"Clear the pelvis." He cleared his throat, turned and walked a few steps to the foot of my bed. He seemed to be distancing himself in every way.

Then, straightening up, he faced Matthew again. From the safety of his familiar role he launched into a lengthy explanation, a little bit as if he were lecturing students. He kept using academic language that didn't address Matthew's anxiety at all . . . was that his way of coping with his discomfort? *Was* he, too, suffering?

"A total pelvic clearance . . . " he began. I did not listen. With my knowledge as a midwife, I did not need an explanation anyway. He was saying only what I expected. He meant a hysterectomy, although I noticed that he did not bring himself to use the word. "Total pelvic clearance" sounded more remote.

A host of different emotions welled up inside me, each one shouting for my attention. I lay back on the pillows numbly, allowing the whole wretched conversation to go over my head.

They could have been discussing someone else, any old patient. Where was their care and concern? Had it been completely swallowed up in the unspoken rivalry between the two specialists? I could have been Exhibit A, a useful example of what the professor was explaining. And Matthew could have been a young schoolboy being bombarded with facts.

"You'll have to understand that if we go ahead, this means no children. Removing a uterus means removing all child-bearing potential."

It was ridiculous. As if we didn't know! And with that choice of words I felt like a cow, a machine, anything but a person. I wanted to scream, "Stop it! I have feelings; haven't you?" But maybe – I wonder, with hindsight – maybe it was precisely *because* he found it so hard that the professor adopted his unfortunate manner. Maybe he felt safer if he sounded objective, clinical, and detached.

The following weeks are blurred in my mind. I have probably subconsciously blotted out some of what happened in order to try to reduce the sting from some of the memories. In a sense, this was the end for me: at least, it was the end of a very great deal . . . so many hopes, so many dreams, so many expectations. Yet it was also the beginning of the end of more important things too. The profound illness that had engulfed me for the four months since February would always leave its scar, but its terrifying intensity was soon to recede.

Only a few things haunt me still, standing out as they do among what, otherwise, my mind refuses to recall. One is the terrible waiting, waiting for the appointed day of operation. In the wake of that most uncomfortable atmosphere between himself and the professor, Richard had made a resolve not to carry out this operation without the professor. He knew how much the professor's opinion was disadvantaged if he could rely only on histology reports. He needed to make his own clinical judgement too: in other words, to see for himself the state of my abdomen and be given the broader view to assess the situation for himself. Only by this means would Richard's judgement be vindicated – something he determined would happen. He was, after all, a consultant and not a mere student.

I was caught in the midst of the friction. The proposed

operation seemed to serve as an opportunity for the two consultants to continue their duel. However much I may have understood the reasoning, that waiting (which turned out to be two whole weeks) felt incredibly hard because I was so weak physically and, increasingly, emotionally too.

At last the day dawned and the activity around me increased as the preparations for my operation began. I knew so well the humiliating procedures which heralded surgery.

"You mustn't drink anything now, Mrs Grayshon." The nurses were busily sticking tubes everywhere – yes, everywhere.

"I'm just going to give you a little enema, Mrs Grayshon."

Little? I thought.

"I'm just going to put a little tube into your bladder, Mrs Grayshon." Why did they keep using the word "little"? To try to make the overall problem seem smaller?

"I'm just going to give you a little shave, Mrs Grayshon."

Everything they did was all so familiar to me. I'd travelled this way so often before, I could have spoken their words of "reassurance" myself. Instead of listening to them, I contemplated the one word that hung over me as a possible outcome of all these preparations: "hysterectomy". To my ears, as a sister, the word was mere information. I would hear it several times a day, or read it on the theatre list pinned to the notice-boards to inform staff of each day's programme. As a sister, it was a word my eyes would scan and register simply as a means of calculating how long patients would be away from the ward. As a patient, however, and especially one aged 25, the word was more than information, and its meaning was anything but routine or everyday. The consequences would remain with me for the rest of my life and, contrary to my expectation, the impact upon me would grow with time rather than diminish.

When, finally, the waiting was over, I lay in the anaesthetic room before being put to sleep. Wherever I looked,
my eyes seemed to fall upon something which held night-
marish memories for me. The trolley with a ventilator
reminded me of when I could not breathe for myself; the
clear bottles of drugs seemed to reinforce that this was my
seventh operation; the needles seemed poised ready to
inflict once again that feeling of vulnerability which I dread
with every anaesthetic.

My eyes closed to try to escape the memories.
Apprehensively I speculated once again on the outcome of
this operation. The form on which I had signed my consent
had read: "Exploratory laparotomy [meaning a jolly good
look inside my abdomen] and maybe proceed to total pelvic
clearance." Would things be bad enough for that, I wondered? Or was I slightly better now? Because if they found
that the infection had resolved I would have to face the logi-
cal conclusion: that I had little reason for complaining still
of pain. If that were the case, then the "good news" would
be blighted by my worst fear, namely that I would then be
proved to have been fussing about nothing. I would be
proved to be a sissy.

Richard had already gone through to the theatre. When I
had seen him, he was twisting his fingers together as if
apprehensive. His professional expertise was about to be
exposed on the operating table. Would he be vindicated in
his boss's eyes?

I rubbed the cold sweat from my hands on the skimpy
sheet draped over me. How I longed for this waiting to end!

The professor swept in. Through the haze of my pre-med
injection I hardly recognized him at first, disguised in his
theatre garb. His breezy manner was the first surprise to
me, but I was even less prepared for the positive shock to
follow.

"Ah well," he chuckled. "The truth will out now, eh?"

It was enough of a struggle to distinguish his distinctive accent from behind his green face-mask but, once I did, I could hardly believe my ears.

"Pardon?" I asked, astonished.

"I say, the truth will out now!" he repeated. He added something about my looking bright-eyed and bushy-tailed – referring, I suppose, to one of my defence mechanisms.

I was totally stunned. Was he saying, directly, that he thought I was a fraud? At such a time as this?

No sooner had the question raced into my mind than the theatre's swing-door banged closed. He had gone. The anaesthetist had taken my arm and was already injecting his drug. The black rubber door squeaked open again. Richard popped his head round, only his dark eyes showing between mask and hat. They crinkled with a reassuring smile.

"See you in there," I heard him say. The buzzing in my ears dragged me into an oppressive sleep.

From a great distance someone was calling me.

"Jane?"

My body was too heavy.

"Jane?"

My breathing felt laboured.

"Jane?"

Oh, I was so weary.

"Can you hear me, Jane?"

Yes, I could hear. But I didn't want to hear. I was too tired. She couldn't have realized how badly I needed to sleep. Who was "she" anyway?

I was standing in a field. I could smell flowers, growing among the corn. They were stale. Every breath I took brought with it the stale smell. It was nauseating. Why was it not sweet? I breathed again.

I tried to turn away from the field of flowers. Whichever way I turned, it stretched ahead of me. I could not get away from it. And the smell once again swept over me. I had to draw another breath. It seemed I was filled with the foul smell. I was very sick.

Something cold and metallic was pushed under my chin. What was this? Perhaps I was not alone. Why could I not see anyone else?

The air was putrid now. If only I could escape the smell! I did not understand, then, that it was my own breath, heavy with the anaesthetic gases, which was inescapable.

"Jane? Can you take a big breath for me?" I wondered why I should want to take a big breath? That would increase the oppressive smell. It was enough to take my little gasps.

The voice altered. "Better give more oxygen," it whispered. A mask was pushed over my face. Its plastic aroma mingled with the stale flowers in my field. It made me feel even more trapped.

"You've had your operation, dear."

My operation? Oh . . . oh, yes, I remember . . . my operation. That's right. Well, what had they found then? What had they done?

My questions faded as I drifted back to the field. The next minute (or so it seemed) I was being bumped and battered. I must be on a trolley, I realized. Dit-dit. Lift doors were crashed open. Dit-dit. Two more wheels crashed over the threshold into the lift. Whirrrrr. The doors were opened again. Dit-dit. Dit-dit.

"You're back in the ward now, Jane." It was the friendly sister speaking. I nodded silently, my eyes still closed. Gradually my field faded, giving way to the slow assimilation of what was actually happening.

I tried to ask questions. "What . . . ?" But I could not articulate properly.

The sister bent over me. She seemed to have insight into how I felt, or at least she used her imagination. She was the sensitive kind of nurse.

"It's all over, Jane."

Oh, if only that were true, I thought. And what had they actually found? What had they done?

"What . . . ?" I repeated. That seemed to be the only word I could muster.

Sister understood. She was a gem.

"They did what they feared they would have to do." Her discretion never faltered. Despite the "rule" that the professor ought to have been the one to tell me, she also honoured my readiness to hear now.

I had had a hysterectomy.

I nodded again, and drifted back to my field.

It was the professor's presence that I remember next. He had entered rather more stealthily than his confident approach in the anaesthetic room before theatre. He commented professionally on the operation, repeating to me their findings. Mostly things have blurred into a smudge of a memory now. Only one of his remarks do I remember. He asked with a completely innocent air, "I expect you were in pain beforehand, weren't you, Jane?"

In pain? What could I say? Pain seemed such an understatement of what I had experienced, such a shallow word for such depth of agony. After all, I had felt that I would die.

"I was, a little," I replied distantly. Words would not have conveyed what my heart knew, so I decided not try.

I was much more alert a few days later when Richard came again to discuss things with me. He did not hide his astonishment at my progress as I stood up proudly. "The discomfort from this operation is nothing, compared . . . " I remarked with glee.

"You just be careful," he warned, but I could see from the gleam in his eye that he was also extremely relieved to see my progress.

I had my questions for him, too.

"Which one of you decided?" I asked, intrigued to learn how the dynamics had resolved between the two surgeons.

"Neither of us," came the cool, measured reply. "As soon as we'd opened you up, there was no question in either of our minds. The decision lay staring up at us on the table."

Then Richard's face suddenly twinkled. "By the way, I got the histology report back today," he told me. "It reads, 'Normal tissue'."

For a second I was confused. How could it have been "normal" when Richard had only just that minute assured me how necessary it had been to remove everything because it had looked so bad?

"Oh?" I looked up at him questioningly. Suddenly I saw the mischief in his dimple, and I understood. It *was* confusing. My medical condition was confusing because some questions remained unanswered. But that was not a reason to dismiss or minimize my pain. This was an occasion when the apparent contradictions needed to be held together with respect and tenderness, which presented a profound challenge to us all.

"I've put the report on the professor's desk," Richard ended. I would like to write that we both smiled as we shared the irony in dignified silence, but it is nearer the truth to admit that one wink from Richard led us both to collapse into a fit of the most undignified giggles. If truth be told, we were probably quite vindictive, having contained the unspoken tension for so long.

The fragility of my newfound confidence was exposed, however, when, one evening I experienced another painful, although different, interaction. The nurse in charge of the ward was one whom I knew, having worked with her elsewhere, and we both found the new dynamic slightly awkward.

She bounded gaily into the room and I prickled immediately, interpreting her breezy manner as insensitive when I

needed tender, loving care. Of course, I hated being so
needy – especially for things that were such emotional non-
sense as that! – and I wouldn't admit to these needs, even to
myself, for about 20 years. Instead I put a great deal of energy into trying to appear "brave" – although in fact I was
quite the opposite of brave. I was denying that I was hurting. To have been brave would have called for me to receive
my real needs with understanding and without despising
myself as a "sissy". I found that too hard at the time.

I was vaguely aware of my vulnerability, like any patient
in hospital, and perhaps especially those who have to
expose their private parts to be viewed and reviewed several times a day. Perhaps that nurse had happened to come
in when I had just begun to dare to *feel* how I was: somewhat low. I was summoning my courage to look at, and
ponder over, what had actually happened to me. I had had
a hysterectomy. I tried to whisper the word to myself
because the only phrase used by anyone in hospital was
"total pelvic clearance". While that was accurate, it gave no
indication of my loss.

Just as I was allowing the first waves of realization of
what a hysterectomy meant to penetrate my heart, the
nurse swept into my room. She marched over to the window beside my bed and briskly swished the curtains across
to shut out the darkness of the approaching night.

"I heard you had your hyst., dear," she said, smiling
broadly.

I felt crushed. Her words seemed to grate on my very
soul. I didn't know what to say, or where to look. I only
recall the urgency with which I wanted to pick up the jug of
cold water from my locker and pour it right over her head.

I lacked compassion at the time, but now I realize that
the nurse must have been at a loss to know what to say or
how to cope with my suffering. And I in my turn did not
recognize her pain. I mistook it for thoughtlessness. More

likely, she felt extremely uncomfortable and covered that pain by what she termed "a bit of light-hearted fun".

Over and over again, my pain caused others to suffer with me . . . Matthew, doctors, nurses. Family and friends who cared for me had their pain, too. They wanted me to be well, and I wasn't. All too easily there would be a cycle of hurt, of self-protection, of hiding lest we be hurt further. Occasionally I felt hurt by silences, not recognizing that they often concealed others' care. But shortly afterwards, a letter from a friend, Geoff, seemed to explain the whole cycle and helped me to understand much better:

> Your suffering is painful to many, Jane, and they cannot cope because they love you so much. It is *because* of the pain that they cannot express the depth of love that they are longing to share with you and which you are longing to receive. Accept the love of many, for it exists, and be motivated to live for the sake of all those who cry out but make no sound.

Such a profound insight: "those who cry out but make no sound". I have discovered that there are many such people in this world. I used to think that those who made no sound had forsaken me. Geoff taught me to look beyond what people say – or fail to say. No one suffers in isolation.

As the days progressed to weeks I began to recover. I could see relief on the faces of those who had suffered with me through this long trial. Everyone was rejoicing. Yet still I was weak – something to which I continued to feel "allergic" – and I could not run away from the consequent limitations. So, deep in my heart, there remained a question. I had missed the boat to heaven, hadn't I? And heaven would have been a better place where, according to the Bible's promise, "there is no more pain".

Was it not true, therefore, that "to die is gain"?

PART TWO

Living in Pain

CHAPTER FOUR

"TO LIVE IS CHRIST AND TO DIE IS GAIN"

Philippians 1:21

As soon as I began to be convalescent, rather than ill, I wanted to embrace life as a gift. The inescapable reality, however, was that for much of the time my body felt like a heavy weight for me to carry around: a burden to my otherwise carefree spirit. At least, that was how I thought of it at the time because I had no concept, then, of my body being true to my spirit and to the whole of me. I thought my body was a burden *despite* my spirit. I had a lot to learn about further, hidden battles that I – and others – may be fighting subconsciously and how that struggle can be reflected in a weariness of the body.

My abdominal infection was certainly eradicated by the hysterectomy, which brought immense relief in every sense. Unfortunately, however, I wasn't completely cured as I might have hoped. I have needed further operations in the years since 1980 and surgery has its cost because, where the body heals, so adhesions form as part of the natural healing mechanism. This means that an area of intestine can become tangled around itself at any time and in varying degrees of severity as it moves. If ever the "tangle" tightens into a sort of knot around the adhesions, it causes a complete obstruction to the normal workings, and the bowel often needs to be freed surgically. That was certainly my situation and for about twelve years I was caught on a knife-edge between bearing the horrible symptoms of pain and nausea, and hoping (often in vain) that they would not become bad enough for me to need another operation.

Another operation . . . and another. The words are so simply written, but each time, they represent a particular experience of seemingly unending suffering. I feel I have a nightmare which can keep repeating itself. Only, I do not dream each time. I have to live it.

And therein lies my agony. If it were a nightmare, I would hope to waken up and discover the freedom of the pain's absence. How often that has been my greatest longing! How often have I longed that the pain might go! The cost of living has seemed to be too high. I do not think it is a surprise for me to admit that I have felt that to die would indeed be gain for me.

Am I being ungrateful for the progress that I have received? It sounds so. Could I not count my blessings (as I had drummed into me as a child!) and discover the freedom of being cheered by God himself? Well, I tried, and hard, but the honest answer is frankly, no. I had experienced God's light in the darkness of desperate illness. I knew the serenity I had experienced when I was close to death, and that could only have been from God. But whenever I have begun to get better from an episode, whether from surgery or "simply" from a bout of bad pain, the dynamics have changed from drama to tedium. The change is depressing, from an *event* of acute agony to a *situation* of humdrum, ongoing pain. Each time I have to face how limited my recovery seems to be. "Better" ends up meaning "improved", but I keep wanting it to mean "well"! This situation meant that I felt imprisoned by pain. Where was the light in that darkness? How *could* a life like that rejoice in

Christ's love or reflect his light? That's what I wanted to know, because that was what I knew to be God's call, supported by his promises.

I know that I am not alone with my questions. Others – many others – in this life long for release. Some do not manage to hang on and they take their own lives. Others endure feeling utterly entrenched in and surrounded by their own form of pain – physical, mental, emotional, spiritual.

Some years ago while I was feeling particularly trapped by my whole situation, a lady whom I knew a little suddenly collapsed. Within a fortnight, she had died. At the funeral I watched her husband and three teenage children. Their faces, though mourning, were serenely radiant. They were confident that Sylvia was now with her Lord, in a place where she knew no more pain, no more tears.

"I mustn't long for that," I told myself. I clenched my fists tightly inside my coat pocket. I wonder whether, after once having contemplated taking one's own form of release, the temptation becomes all the more powerful.

I looked at the wooden coffin. It was as if it were insignificant, nothing. It reminded me of a book I had read in which the Little Prince had described a dead body. "Like an old abandoned shell," he had said. "There is nothing sad about old shells . . . "

No, there was nothing sad about Sylvia's dead body. Those who were left were sad in their loss, of course, but not Sylvia. She had only gained. It was not the coffin which was difficult for me to look at. It was myself.

I was still encased in my body, my pain. I was like that Little Prince before his death. He had said, "I cannot carry this body with me. It is too heavy." That was how I felt too.

That day, I felt particularly burdened by the heaviness of my body. I had hoped that, as a result of seeing a new specialist in London a week or so previously, a new treatment might have been suggested to alleviate my symptoms. I had thought a clever new "bigwig" might be able to cure me. I could not have been more mistaken. The consultation had hardly begun before that hope was torn from me. "You're a problem," were the doctor's first words to me. "What do you expect but pain, with a history like yours?"

Sylvia's funeral service was too soon after that for me. I was not able to cope with the stark comparison between the old abandoned shell in the coffin and my living body, pulsating with pain.

Throughout the service I wrestled with myself. While others wept silently in sorrow, I fought back my tears. I had to keep control. I knew that if I had begun to shed one tear, that might have opened a chink in the wall I had built up like a dam to hold back my lake of unshed tears. Then I would not have had just a quiet little sniffle. Once my wall was breached I would have sobbed uncontrollably. I would have been beside myself; I would have wept on and on. My fear was – indeed, it still remains as I write this, many years on – that the tears could one day overwhelm me, prostrate me under the weight of them.

"I can't bear this, Lord. I can't. I can't!" I would have cried. "What are you asking of me? What are you doing to me? It's too much! If pain is to be my whole life, I don't want it. I don't want life!"

All this was pent up inside me during the funeral. The fight to keep control was enormous.

And it was not just on my own behalf that I felt distraught. "Lord, look at Matthew, quietly bearing so much. When I look at his eyes, I see reflected in them the whole story of my suffering. I feel helpless. I am the main character acting out this saga, yet I have no means of altering the plot. Lord, stop it, please!"

But I didn't let go like that. I couldn't: neither in public nor even in private. I would have frightened even myself, I think, by how much I would have cried. There's a sense in which I have only just begun my weeping. Back then at Sylvia's funeral I managed somehow – somehow – to maintain some composure and some unselfish serenity. It was so hard! At that moment everything seemed hard: all my pain . . . life itself . . . Even God seemed harsh, if I were honest.

And there, all the time, stood that coffin. Dead. Nothing was hard any more for that old abandoned shell. To die was gain.

I burned with the frustration that this, so nearly, had been me. Not once, but at least three times I had nearly died. I had not been afraid at the time. Yet seeing that coffin opened my mind to the memories like turning on a tap. Indeed, as we rose to sing the next hymn at Sylvia's funeral, the vivid pictures of those occasions flooded back to me in their full horror. They rushed into my mind with the clarity of a video film in my brain. I felt as if I had just stood myself under a gushing waterfall, rather than simply stood up to sing in a church.

Uppermost was a time in 1979 when I had been on the operating table in theatre. I became aware that I was able to hear all that was going on around me. For a reason I could not fathom at the time, I was amazingly detached, as if I were an interested observer of everything. That was the effect of the anaesthetic. Fascinated, I listened to the tense voices that surrounded me.

"She needs more oxygen."

"Her pulse rate is very high."

"Her blood pressure's dropped even further."

Then a man's authoritative boom. "Get some plasma. Quickly, nurse." The sound of wooden clogs on the stone floor receded, running, then returned.

"Where *is* the plasma?" she had asked, flustered.

Poor soul, I mused dreamily, remembering my own early days as a student nurse learning the whereabouts of equipment on each ward or department.

The man's voice in reply was raised. "I don't care where the h*** it is. Just get it. Quickly!"

I felt detached from all this. I was interested in speculating why they should want the plasma so quickly for me. I could also have told her exactly where the plasma was and, illogically of course, I wanted to pass on the information. "On the second shelf, above the dextrose solution," I wanted to say helpfully. But it didn't matter. All this was going on, but it didn't seem to affect me somehow. I felt unburdened. Why were they worrying? I felt amazingly free and light.

"She's not breathing." It was the man's voice. What did it matter, I thought? I felt fine.

"Blood pressure's very low." They didn't seem to understand that I could hear, and I wondered why not.

"Speed up that drip!" came a command with an edge of urgency. Really, they were fussing. Certainly they couldn't have known how well I felt.

"Jane? Jane?" A voice calling me kept intruding upon my freedom. "Can you take a big breath for me, Jane?"

No, I couldn't. Why bother anyway? I was flying, floating, free.

"Pass the laryngoscope." That was the man's voice again.

Suddenly my chin was jerked upwards. Fingers pressed my jaw and throat. An enormous metal instrument was being pushed into my mouth, past my tonsils. I couldn't get away from it. I couldn't shout for help.

The fiddling stopped, but their invasion into me had hardly begun. Involuntarily I felt myself drawing breath. Or was it a breath? A heaviness fell upon me, infusing my whole being. Then, as suddenly as they had filled, my lungs emptied.

"Good," came the voice. Good? I thought. The man was so wrong. This was not "good". I felt much worse now. I resented the heaviness, the burden of breathing. His interference had ended the feeling of a freedom and lightness which I had experienced for the first time ever. I resented it deeply. I felt claustrophobic, trapped, pressed in by the tubes now being tied into my mouth with a bandage around my head.

Then I heard the click-hum of another machine. As its hum crescendoed, I felt my lungs fill again. Click-hum. They emptied. A new horror came over me. With a chill, I realized I had been put on to a ventilator.

In church, the hymn singing ended at the same time as this memory finished replaying itself in my mind. I turned my eyes once again towards Sylvia's family. They too had become sickeningly familiar with the distinctive click-hum of a ventilator. Sylvia's breathing had also needed to be assisted for a number of days before she had died.

I wanted to be able to reassure them. "There's no terror in actually dying," I would have said. "You just feel ill. It's like feeling ill with flu, except that you don't get better just temporarily. Once you die you become completely whole and well. Your mum will be face to face with Jesus now. Permanently."

The prospect of being face to face with Jesus was something for which I continued to crave. On each occasion that I have felt close to dying, I have been conscious of Jesus very close to me: so close that I know how unsurprised I would have been if his presence had become a physical thing. I could envisage him reaching out to take my hand. For onlookers I am sure that that would have been the moment that we call death; but for me it would have been the beginning of Life in a big way.

That led my thoughts to an occasion when I had so looked forward to Jesus coming to take me by the hand. I had been at Matthew's theological college when a guest preacher had visited. This was in February 1980, just before my collapse. He had shared with all the students in chapel that evening a picture he had envisaged during the prayers. He felt it was a gift from God and that it was describing the scene that lay ahead for "somebody present". He described to us how Jesus was leading "God's daughter" into heaven as a bride. Angels were forming a corridor as they stood waiting to see the Bridegroom come to lead his bride down that angelic corridor. All the angels were craning their necks to see the beauty of the bride. Oh, how vividly I could receive that picture and see Jesus' enormous pride as he led his bride to stand beside him before his Father!

At the time of hearing this man's vision, none of us had any idea, of course, of what lay ahead during the college year. Matthew and I did know that his words might come to have a very special ring of truth for us personally.

As I contemplated Sylvia's death, the idea of being welcomed into heaven was all immensely reassuring. But I found it was no use comparing my pain with others'. Sylvia's suffering had been so worthwhile. It had led her to her death, when she would see God face to face. She could be thankful even for the actual pain, because it was acting as a vehicle to carry her to the place where God would "wipe away every tear".

But for me? I desperately hoped those prophetic words, speaking of the release of death into fullness and wholeness of life, were for me. But contemplating them only seemed to heighten the distress of living on, burdened by so much pain. St Paul wrote of his own life, "For me to live is Christ and to die is gain." His life was no idyll; he hadn't written the first phrase from some millionaire's paradise island. *That* is not heaven on earth. He knew how to live closely united to Christ in heaven while still in the drudgery of earth. He wrote those very words from prison while he had been chained to a guard, with all the humiliation that involved in matters of daily personal hygiene. He was no stranger to suffering, or to unfair treatment and even brutality in prison. The challenge to me of St Paul was for me to join him in his description of life being so securely joined to Christ *here*, and resist taking the escape route of longing for the next truth that seemed so much easier to slide into: "to die is gain". I had no clue how I could "make" myself say, with him, "For me to live is Christ," *and mean it*! I could perhaps have mouthed the words, but they would have been empty, without conviction or sincerity. The vivid truth was that I would have much preferred to "gain" that wonderful welcome into heaven (who wouldn't?!), especially fed by the picture of the corridor of angels craning their necks to see me on Jesus' arm.

Sylvia's release acted as a catalyst for me to long for God's nearness, for the promise of a wonderful, permanent future. It reminded me that my gain would be eternal. I was somewhat shocked to discover in myself a reaction near to bitterness. I had been so near to this wonderful reception in which Sylvia was rejoicing . . . and yet so far. Had I died peacefully and entered triumphantly into God's glory, then I and those around me could at least have seen a purpose to the otherwise unexplained suffering. We do like to know *why* God allows what he does . . .

But that is not what God had planned for me. Jesus did not come to take me by the hand and lead me with joy to his Father. He did not give the release that Matthew and I had discussed together and then anticipated with Colin back in Easter 1980. He did not grant me the sense of satisfaction that he had any purpose at all because, from my point of view, the prolonged illness and almost constant persistent pain seemed *such* a waste of my life – of my vivacity, which could not find expression in this body. Instead, God called me to stay in my shell. He called me to remain, living in pain, for we did not know how long.

Perhaps he leads us gently, but I cannot say he has always felt gentle to me. The jolt of realizing that God wants me to face this second-best place, on earth, can still catch me off-guard and I can feel devastated. At those times, I desperately need to be reassured by God himself that his way and his timing are perfect.

And yet the paradox is that the light shines in the darkness. During the day, the stars, which *are* still shining in the sky, are completely invisible. They need the context of the night sky before they can be seen. People who have never ventured out to sit under the canopy of the night sky have never seen that particular miraculous sight known by those who have. Those who have seen it from being surrounded by deep darkness have seen much more than those who have only viewed it from the safety of a street-lit city. Dangerous though it feels to be in deep darkness, the awesome view from there is incomparable and, when we interpret the spiritual parable, it brings a deep reassurance to one's heart.

I did once receive exactly such reassurance. Lying in hospital one day in 1980, semi-conscious, semi-drugged, I suddenly became aware of a great clarity of mind. I knew without doubt that the thoughts in my head were very important. Reaching for a pen and scrap of old tissue paper, I began to write, phrase by phrase. I did not know the next sentence until I had written the first. I believe that God was directly giving me his words of comfort for the darkness that was to follow:

Jane, you long for the end (of your life) because you long for heaven. That is where you know that I, the Sovereign Lord, will be. You think of death as the end. There is in fact a different kind of end: the end of your resources. That is where you cannot cope, you cannot bear any more. That is also where I am, at that "end". Naturally you cannot feel me there because of the overwhelming nature of feeling unable to bear a moment more with this earth's pain.

Therefore, prepare yourself for arriving at the end of your own strength. First, recognize that it exists – that you will feel desperate and that you will be lonely. Then, while you are cool and rational, see ahead that I *shall* be there. This is my promise, to be with you *always*.

Do not consider this to mean that I shall act, or be seen to act, when your darkness descends. Only, when it comes, remember that this is the end of your coping, and that that is where I take over, silently, without you even knowing.

I do not expect you to look forward to these times, nor to look back on them with joy. But you needn't dread them so much, knowing that I understand. Do not forget my hour in Gethsemane.

Arriving home after Sylvia's funeral, I raced upstairs. I thumbed through my drawer of precious pieces of paper until I found these words. Hungrily, I read them over and over again. Yes, that was one of those times about which God had spoken as if in anticipation of the very day. I felt at the end of my resources, unable to cope, yet I had specific help. I believe that those words of comfort were from God. Certainly they have proved to be a comfort for me many, many times whenever darkness has threatened to envelop me completely.

Christ is not only to be found in death. I relaxed a little as I opened my mind to God's promise: no matter *how* bad I felt nor *how* much I couldn't feel him, he was *always* with me. This was his promise, his absolute assurance, however hard that felt for me to believe.

The gospel does not only tell of Jesus rescuing people *from* their suffering. There is a way in which he can rescue us *through* it, even during pain's occasional furnace-like intensity. He can also rescue us *in* it. If God's will was for me to live, then Christ was to be found there as well. I sense a gentleness in the text of the Bible whenever Jesus spoke about suffering. He described himself as a "good shepherd" who is so concerned when even one sheep gets lost, that he will go and tramp the moors until he finds it. He described to his disciples how, after finding it, he would draw it into his divine embrace. The prophet Isaiah foretold this (in chapter 40, verse 11) and even painted a picture of *how*, exactly, the shepherd would reach down to carry his lambs, and how he would lead his sheep:

> He tends his flock like a shepherd:
>> He gathers the lambs in his arms
> and carries them close to his heart;
>> he gently leads those that have young.

I take such comfort from these promises. When we cannot walk, God will lift us and carry us, like lambs whom he bends down to touch. "He gathers the lambs in his arms and carries them close to his heart." What a privilege for us to be snuggled, by him, in such an honoured place!

There is a different message for us when we *can* walk, when we are able to be responsible, like the sheep who have the responsibility to care for their young: "he gently leads those that have young." I think we may be allowed to interpret this to include us when we are adults and find that our "child" self, our "little" self, has peeped through. We are responsible for the part of ourself which is like a child. I am referring to the times when we may feel embarrassingly young and vulnerable and silly – because we have glimpsed our own hurt "child". We don't usually notice until afterwards, when we shudder to realize that we've behaved like a child, or spoken like a child, or become angry like a child. Those are the occasions, I believe, when Jesus understands how adults are made, and we can trust him to lead us: "he gently leads those that have young." The text affirms most beautifully that, far from punishing us for being immature, God still looks upon us with loving respect, whatever state we are in. There is no suggestion of impatience or him chivvying us to hurry up and "grow up".

Back on the day of Sylvia's funeral I knelt before God with my Bible, absorbed by the beauty of God's assurances. I continued exploring, turning next to the beatitudes. "How blest are those who know their need of God", I read from the slightly different translation of the *New English Bible*. That was me all right; I knew my need of God. "The kingdom of Heaven is theirs."

"The kingdom of Heaven *is* mine!" I closed my eyes and repeated to myself. I wanted to absorb every piece of consolation or promise.

Then there was one of my favourite psalms: "As the deer pants for streams of water, so my soul pants for you, O God" (Psalm 42:1). This verse certainly summarized my longing. But I longed for yet more than the nebulous, unseen Spirit of God. I wanted to *see* love, to *feel* tenderness, from God. Turning to the book of Isaiah, I began to read from chapter 43. I lifted my head and closed my eyes. I tried to absorb the love of God as I pondered his word.

To trust this verse was, I was sure, the only way I could endure living here on earth, in pain. If I could really receive this verse as God himself speaking to me here and now, I would be able to know without doubt not only that "to die is gain", but also, as the more challenging half of the verse says, "to live is Christ".

In silence I remained kneeling, alone before God, waiting in silence to allow that special miracle to happen if God willed: for his word to speak to me personally.

"You are precious, and honoured in my sight, and I love you."

CHAPTER FIVE

"YOU ARE PRECIOUS"

Isaiah 43:4

Within a few months of my "total pelvic clearance", the fog that had seemed to envelop me began to clear, allowing our confidence to grow in the fact that the surgeons had indeed successfully stopped the downward spiral of my illness. I was gradually regaining health and strength. Although I had a secret, niggling fear that something was still lacking, nevertheless I looked forward with eager anticipation to a visit to a convent where Matthew and I could retreat from the pressures of daily life.

When we arrived at the convent in Hertfordshire, I felt happy enough. We were warmly welcomed by the five Carmelite sisters whom we had first come to know during earlier visits the previous year. They were the Sisters of the Love of God, who saw their calling as spreading God's love throughout the world in prayer. They each sought to let God's love be made bigger in themselves. That love certainly spread to us in the welcome we received. As they showed Matthew and myself to our separate little rooms, I was full of anticipation that our three days there would help me to feel restored in every way.

We discussed only a few details about the silent meals

and other practical matters before the sisters returned to their own contemplative work. Then, as Sister Rachel-Mary graciously left me in order to "allow me to enjoy the peace and stillness", she closed my door.

Suddenly I felt terribly alone. I had expected to find quietness, rest and peace in the silence. Instead, I found confusion. My mind was full of thoughts all clamouring loudly for my attention.

What was wrong with me? I had made good progress and was well on the way to recovery. I had been seriously ill, on the brink of dying, but I had come through. Why was my heart not full of praise and thankfulness to God? Surely I ought to be rejoicing with all those who had prayed for this healing?

Dissatisfied with myself for not being able to find peace even in so quiet a place, I decided to take a stroll in the extensive grounds. Perhaps being outside would take me out of myself, away from the simplicity of my room.

I sat down on a wooden bench beside the fish-pond. The water glistened in the summer sun. To the right and behind, the kitchen garden stretched down the slope, all methodically laid out with vegetables. Beyond, huge brown nets enclosed further neat rows of fruit bushes. Everything I saw was ordered and calm. Closing my eyes to enjoy the sun's balmy rays, I tried to absorb some of this peacefulness. I heard the sound of the bird-song, interrupted only by the gentle scratching noise of a sister hoeing the well-tilled earth.

I thought back to one of my previous visits to the convent. I had been very pleased with life then. I had been on the crest of a wave with my achievements. I had just been appointed to a good position as a nursing sister doing research. The post had combined both academic and clinical work, alongside the university professor and two consultants. This early promotion stood me in very good stead for my career.

I had also won a national award, given by the Royal College of Nursing for an essay, and had been made to feel very important as a special guest at a cocktail party in the rather grand atmosphere of the Royal College in London. The award had led to a contract for me to write a nursing textbook. At the age of 24 I felt thrilled and honoured. I could look at what I'd done and believe I had a valuable contribution to make in life. Through my achievements, I felt that my life was worthwhile and that therefore I was precious.

I reflected how much my thinking had changed during that particular weekend at the convent. Having arrived so full of self-worth, suddenly on the first morning I'd been brought up with quite a jolt. A note had been pushed under my door. I recognized the handwriting to be Mo's, another student who had come with us from Matthew's college. I opened the envelope to find that she had copied a simple poem – she didn't know where she had found it – but she had written it out specially for me to meditate upon during the course of our silence. This is what I read:

> I wait for you, my child.
> I desire your love
> More than anything else you can give me.
> Not your service
> Not your struggling and trying to please me,
> Or to please others.
> I want you to love me;
> To love me with all your heart, mind, soul, strength.
> This is the first commandment
> And matters more than all else besides.
> I need your love, fellowship, devotion and worship.
> I want you to be single-minded in this one thing.
> My Spirit is within you
> To enable you

To empower you
To fill your heart with love.

I desire this not sometimes
But always.

The poem had absolutely stopped me in my tracks. It suggested to me that God would be more pleased to see my relationship with him deepen, than to see me doing wonderful things with my talents, even though those talents were God-given. "I desire your love more than anything else you can give me" – more, even, than my achievements for him. Who I *was* was more important to him than what I did or achieved in life.

As I recalled that previous stay in the convent, something seemed to slot into place in my mind. Could it be, I wondered as I got up to walk again through the grounds, that I had allowed myself to forget the lessons I had learned through Mo's poem? Had I been lulled back into the way our society thinks of people's worth, and away from God's perspective? That would certainly explain why I felt unhappy with my own company. In strong contrast to the high sense of self-esteem I enjoyed then, I did not now have any "achievements" to be pleased about. I had spent the past six months being passive: during that time I had had no chance to "earn" any feeling of being special in life. Unlike my last visit here, I now had no outward measure that I was precious. All I had done was to endure the illness. I had nothing whatsoever to show for six whole months of my life.

The convent bell, tolling softly, interrupted my musings. Slowly I strolled back up the slope towards the chapel. But my mind did not enter into the ten-minute, chanted office. From there we filed directly into lunch and it was with relief that I remembered that the rule of silence meant that

I was not expected to join in with any polite conversation. I was in no mood to speak: my mind was elsewhere.

I chose a seat in the dining-room from which I could look out to the garden. I felt that that might raise my spirits. Nature seemed so uncluttered by the burdens that appeared to weigh me down.

While we ate in solemn silence, I recalled a day when I was told that I was precious: not by words, but by tears. It was during the four-month crisis earlier in the year. A very dear friend, Jennie, had once again left her young baby in order to journey in to the hospital to be with me. She had known how ill I was and had wanted to show how much she cared.

The day she came was one of my worst. I was so distracted by the burning intensity of pain that I had begun to go into a state of shock. I had lost my way around the familiar ward. In my disorientation I had become confused with my normal bodily functions. The sister had summoned the consultant out of theatre to come to me, because she knew I was going downhill. By the time he had come, I had been unable to respond to his questions. I had just stared through him, as indeed I did to Jennie when she arrived later.

It was a crucial time: the time when, I suspect, I gave up my drive to get well. The consultant, I was later told, was himself distraught about my condition, probably because he knew that no medical man can stop a patient giving up her spirit. He recognized how I felt. He described me as being "on a downward spiral". He knew that I could bear very little more. I was utterly spent. That day, I was simply giving up.

Jennie did not try to cajole me out of my mood with philosophical reasons to live. She simply wept. She must have sensed immediately how I was, and how I felt; for even as she took her coat off I remember seeing her face dissolve. She dragged the nearest chair to be close beside me, took my unresponsive hand in both of hers, and sobbed. She buried her face in her hands, and mine, kissing mine and stroking them as if she were handling a really valuable treasure. Though I must have been quite passive, she let me feel that I was precious.

I thank God Jennie cried as she did. Some people might have suppressed their natural reaction, trying not to add to my problems by parading their distress. But Jennie's tears had a profound and extraordinary effect on me. They spoke to me in a place where words could not reach. I do not understand the mechanism; all I know is that I was enabled to be present with myself in a way that I had lost. Through the gentle simplicity of Jennie's presence, I was led back to a more "normal" state of mind. I had been overwhelmed to the point of giving up; when her sadness spilled out so visibly, I naturally turned to look at her with tenderness . . . which represented my turning to look at *life* once more, and to look upon it with tenderness. The whole interaction was so simple, so natural – yet its effect was pivotal, an example of the deep healing power found in the simplicity of human love.

And Jennie did more than bring me round from my confused state. Her tears showed me that she cared. She caused the first stirrings in me to turn back from my only desire at that moment, which was to avoid more pain. Fear had been dominant and when her gentle love came in, apprehension was replaced with soothing reassurance. Jennie valued me here. She could see that I had given up fighting, and clearly she longed to see me retrieve some of my former spark of life. By her tears, she told me that my life was worthwhile.

This memory was at the same time consoling to me and upsetting. I was consoled to think of Jennie's indisputable love; yet I was perturbed to find that I almost wanted to repeat the whole scene so that I could feel reassured thus once again.

Watching a squirrel darting up a tree outside, I felt I was beginning to understand why I was not particularly thankful to have been saved from dying in hospital. The trouble was, I did not really believe that I was precious – precious to God, precious in the world. Stripped of all worldly reassurance that I was making a valuable contribution to life, now it was apparent that I had lost my sense of self-worth. The spiritual lessons I thought I had learned from Mo's poem were merely words: head knowledge and not heartfelt conviction. Frankly, God's words of comfort had stopped being a true comfort to me. I had lost the reality of his pronouncement, "You are precious and honoured, and I love you." I reacted by saying to God in a rather embarrassed way, "Oh, that's nice of you." But I did not feel any different.

I glanced across to Matthew, who was eating awkwardly from his wooden bowl (each person at the convent used one instead of a china plate). "What was he thinking?" I wondered. He, more than anyone else, was caught up in the cost of my being alive: he was the one who supported me so strongly throughout both the crises and the long-term residual pain. Yet he had never once suggested that the value of my life was not worth the pain, even though he too was caught up in that cost. He did not feel, as I did, that my life was just a burden.

My eyes filled with tears as I thought once again of the burden I felt myself to be: a burden both to myself, enduring pain and feeling unwell, and to others who had to endure my limitations and my moans.

Suddenly I was aware of Sister Rachel-Mary looking at me. I had been so lost in thought that I had forgotten that I was with others. But it was too late. One tear had spilled down my cheek, and she had seen . . .

There was a gentle knock on the door of my room later in the afternoon. I knew then that Sister Rachel-Mary had noticed the signs of my low spirits. She sat on my bed as she asked how I was.

"I don't know," I replied lamely. "I just don't know." I was too bewildered to be objective about myself.

"You've been through a great ordeal," she said with conviction. "A lot has happened to you physically. You need time to catch up emotionally and spiritually."

I smiled and relaxed a little. It was an enormous relief to be accepted so fully. Sister Rachel-Mary was very perceptive and wise. I felt able to trust her with what was weighing so heavily on my heart.

"I know I ought to be grateful to God for healing me," I began tentatively. "But I just don't feel glad to be alive."

Sister Rachel-Mary frowned a little. "Like a death-wish, you mean?"

"No, I don't actively want to die. I'm feeling much more passive than that. I just lack any enthusiasm for living."

"Well, you've been profoundly weakened, Jane: not just physically, but in every way. Anyone is bound to feel like this after being as ill as you have been, quite apart from the pain you're still having to combat every day. You're a strong person. You expect yourself to dance through everything, but you are setting yourself goals which are too high." Her eyes twinkled affectionately.

Comforted a little by her reassurance, I dared to explain further.

"It's not just that, though," I confessed. "This morning I realized that I don't feel that I'm precious." I could not say more, for fear that my voice might reflect my nearness to breaking down.

"Aren't you allowing yourself to forget all the signs from other people who have shown you how precious you are to them? You yourself have written that to me in your letters."

She was right. People had reached out to me in many different ways: from those who sent simple but caring messages by card or with flowers, to those who gave up whole weeks of their time to help run the house.

"Yes, that has helped. But it doesn't stop my underlying feeling that I am now thoroughly restricted in what I can do in life. I mean, it wouldn't really matter if I were no longer in the world. If I had died when we expected me to – well, everyone would have been sad, but they would have got over it. Life would have gone on without me. So, what does it mean, 'You are precious'? Is it important that I am still here?"

I did not confess out loud that, within my own head, I had answered the last question with a screaming "NO!" I looked at her, feeling slightly uncomfortable at having spoken so intimately, but her bowed head signalled that she was ready to listen to more.

"Because as far as I am concerned, it means drilling myself, 'You've GOT to stay alive. You MUST battle on. Trust God. Keep going. God says it's worth your being alive so you HAVE to believe him.' But it's hard . . . it's so hard." My voice trailed away.

There was a silence between us; but I knew that Sister Rachel-Mary was not dependent on words for communication. The serenity in her face encouraged me to open up even more.

"The trouble is, I suppose, that my self-esteem is either built up or eroded by other people's image of me. I work my guts out trying to be noticed as doing well, be it at work or among friends or in the church fellowship. I enjoy giving of myself because that is very fruitful: it gives me the feedback that my role in life is appreciated, according to what I give. Being appreciated makes me feel precious."

Sister Rachel-Mary nodded with understanding. As part of her vocation she had schooled herself in yielding her own desires and ambitions and offering them to God. That was the synthesis of the three vows she had made when she became a nun: poverty, chastity, and obedience.

"This illness has forced me into a place where I can't give as I would like. I am forced instead to receive. You mentioned just now about all the care I've been shown. Perhaps people imagine that I must feel precious because I receive so much kindness from those who want to minister to me. But I'm so accustomed to 'earning' my feeling of being precious that I find it difficult to stop giving and simply, passively, to receive."

Already I was feeling better for talking all this out. I could almost guess her "answer" before Sister Rachel-Mary spoke.

"But our Lord does not think of importance and specialness as we do. He wants us to learn that we are precious to him in whatever state we are in. He values us for who we are in the quietness of our soul."

I was silenced, at last, by the wisdom of her words. Then, before leaving me to rest once more, Sister Rachel-Mary asked me to think about a verse. I knew it well: Psalm 46, verse 10, "Be still, and know that I am God."

"Spend time with it," she said confidently. "It may well help you now."

I thought at first that it was rather an obvious verse for her to quote to me. What else was I doing at the convent other than "being still"? Yet I admired Sister Rachel-Mary greatly, and I knew that after her years of a close pilgrimage with her Lord, anything she said was worth my taking seriously.

Whatever I did, I held the verse in my mind . . . brushing my teeth, eating my meals, kneeling quietly before the cross in the little chapel. The next day in my reading I found a Latin translation of the same verse: *Vacete et videte* – "Vacate, make empty, and see . . . " I looked pensively to the huge log fire beside me.

"So," I told myself, "this is the key. I've to empty out all the things which lead to my self-satisfaction. I've to count them as trash instead of treasures. God is not interested in my achievements. I've to come to him with nothing. He wants only me, in my emptiness. Only then can he do what he wills in me."

During the following months, I kept these thoughts uppermost in my mind. I found myself much less despondent whenever I was faced with the limitations set by the continuing low-level pain. Then at Christmas time, another dear friend confirmed my thoughts about "doing" and "being". Sally wrote in her Christmas letter: "In writing this letter about the 'doings' of the year, one is tremendously aware that these are only the icing on the cake, and that the all-important work is that of the Spirit of God working within our lives."

As I look back, I know that the Spirit of God, working within me, has taken away much of my "doing". He has worked like a gardener pruning a valuable plant or tree, in that he has not merely cut out dead or useless growth: he has also cut me where I have been fruitful and growing healthily. This is exactly what Jesus said, "*Every* branch that does bear fruit he prunes, that it may bear more fruit" (italics mine; John, chapter 15).

To find areas of my life being cut out by God has sometimes been hard. At times I have felt that he has been so ruthless in his pruning, and it has hurt so much, that I could not be precious to him. But I know that that is not true. Again, it is a poem, whose author I don't even know, which has helped me to see beyond the hurt of what God has taken away from me, and to trust that he has a loving purpose:

> It is the branch that bears the fruit
>   that feels the knife
> To prune it for a larger growth,
>   a fuller life . . .

It is the hand of Love Divine
   that holds the knife,
That cuts and breaks with tenderest touch,
That thou, whose life has borne some fruit
   May'st now bear much.

Whatever pain my Father has asked me to endure is not worthless or without a loving purpose – however unloving it all seems at times. I should not be surprised, nor should my faith waver, when some fruitful area of my life is cut away. But that is easier for me to write about than to endure. No amount of acceptance diminishes the dreadful reality of suffering.

Sometimes it is hard to discern when the Spirit of God is at work, and where his enemy is endeavouring to destroy. They may both want to cut away fruitful areas of my life, but for very different reasons. My Father only takes something away in order to make room for fuller growth. His enemy might take the same thing away as a means of tempting me to become bitter, resentful and self-pitying.

I have needed to trust my Father never to cut anything out of my life except with loving hands which tend the wounds where he has pruned. His purpose is never to destroy because, he says clearly, "you are precious". He cares for me. I know this, though if I am honest I have to admit that I do not, as yet, really feel the tenderness of his love. Indeed, the more time goes on, the more I realize that I have *further* to go along that path – I used to think I was almost there! Now I am beginning to think that it is a life-long journey. Perhaps the whole purpose of our being here is to know, fully, the tenderness of his love. In a film, *Moulin Rouge*, released in 2001, the philosophy repeated over and over, literally from the opening scene to the closing one, is "The best thing in life is to love and be loved in return". I could not disagree more. I am convinced that the best thing in life is to discover that we do not have to love God before he will love us. Even if we remain nasty and horrible, God loves us with lavish extravagance. We are loved no matter what we do, or fail to do. Nothing *can* separate us from God's love. Nothing. We are of infinite value to him. We are precious to him beyond words.

We are barely able to understand such good news; we need time for it to penetrate our souls. Thankfully, God helps us by his Holy Spirit who whispers into our souls; his very names speak volumes: the Comforter, and Wonderful Counsellor.

As we journey along our pathway through whatever kind of pain we know, there are times when the practical outworking of the Spirit of God within our lives can seem very, very hard. We hope that, since God is the Comforter, he will have comforted us before we've suffered enough for us even to fathom what's wrong. Then we find that God isn't in such a rush as we are, and that hurts. He doesn't seem to be so good at comforting after all. Or we hope that, as he is the Wonderful Counsellor, we will hear his voice clearly. Then we realize that we have no idea whether we are listening to the voice of his counsel or whether we're clinging on to wishful thinking. We find we have a whole journey alongside our Shepherd in order for us to learn to fulfil what he promised us, that his sheep will know his voice. That takes practice, and time. Suddenly the "wonder" has gone from our hope for the Wonderful Counsellor to tell us all the answers on the spot.

Often, I have sung the hymn,

> Spirit of the living God
> Fall afresh on me . . .
> Break me, melt me,
> Mould me, fill me . . .

God has answered, and he continues to answer, that prayer-song. He has broken me, and when I have felt the pain of being broken I have reflected on how much easier it is to sing the song than to accept the brokenness.

God has used physical suffering to break me. There are many little reminders in day-to-day life which cause me to think of my body's brokenness and incompleteness. When I see the scars from twelve abdominal operations, I am reminded that my physical brokenness also represents a brokenness of my spirit. Through physical surgery, God has "opened me up" and shown me parts of myself which I may have preferred not to see.

The smallest little thing occasionally reminds me that part of my womanhood has been taken away. For some years, whenever I saw the sales machines in ladies' toilets, for example, I felt slightly less of a woman. I knew I should have been counting my blessings and I was glad of the freedom I had each month, but I also felt left out, incomplete, broken.

God calls all of us to be broken, just as he was broken. In the upper room, Jesus took a whole loaf of bread and broke it into pieces, as a dramatic illustration of what happened to his body. And he asks his disciples to follow him.

God has melted me. I expect I would have welcomed a nice gentle heat to make me aglow with his Spirit, but that would not have been hot enough to melt me. Instead, he has put me through a great burning intensity of heat, just as gold has to be put into a white-hot furnace in order to be melted. When the fire of purification has felt so hot, so painful, I have often wondered why I ever asked God to melt me. Yet I know (in my head) that God has only done this because he values me. He is interested in the quality of my life and he purifies me in the fire – because I am precious.

Looking back, I can see clearly that God has melted away

lots of rubbish from my life, and that, however unbearable, his fire has strengthened my faith, just as Peter wrote, "your faith [is] of greater worth than gold, which perishes even though refined by fire" (1 Peter 1:7). I trust that he has done this in order to remould me.

God is moulding me, and in being moulded I have had to learn to be pliable so he can reshape me as he wants. He keeps on and on, just as a potter persists at his clay. I know that with each successive bout of illness I change a little, as God knocks off another sharp edge from me; but sometimes I feel tired and dizzy going round the potter's wheel. I look at those who do not seem to be having such a hard time, and fall into the trap of self-pity.

Yet I do know that God does not delight in causing his little ones to suffer. He continues to mould me because he is delighted to create vessels according to his design. I am beginning to learn not to wish that I could jump off the wheel, but to give myself more to his hands. I am beginning to pray honestly, "Keep turning your wheel today, so that your hands can mould me as you desire."

Being broken, melted and moulded leaves a vessel which is ready to be filled. At the convent, God convicted me that my value in life to him lies in my emptiness. I knew then that I can only be filled by him when I make space for him, which means emptying myself. The Holy Spirit has had the hard work to do, in me, of breaking my strong exterior, melting me to the core, and moulding me. All his work, which continues, has been in order to fill me.

God has filled me, quietly and undramatically. I know that at times I would have preferred to remain filled than to dare to pray, again and again, for the hurt of being broken, melted, and moulded. But God yearns for me to keep growing, to keep being filled. He wants to keep working in me, because I am precious.

I constantly need to keep readjusting my perspectives. So

much of what I see around me threatens to deceive me with the lie that it is a person's achievements that give him value. Consequently I begin to fear that the debilitating aspects of my suffering rob me of my worth. But God views things differently. He loves me for who I am more than for what I can do. And if it was my very pain that forced me into discovering this deep truth, then surely I should embrace it rather than despise it?

However, there is a tension to be held between this truth and the fact that God is the one who, looking with compassion on his suffering people, said with authority, "Be healed."

CHAPTER SIX

"BE HEALED"

Mark 5:34

God is able to take away all pain. I have no doubt about that. Jesus did many wonderful miracles while he was on earth and I have seen his power at work in the present day. So, I wondered, how about him intervening in my own suffering, and using his healing power to put an end to all my pain?

I knew God could do this. In fact, there is much more of a problem when we believe that God can change difficult situations, but then we face a situation when he doesn't choose to. That is the great mystery of God and suffering: he can do fantastic things at the click of his fingers, but he doesn't always. He isn't like a magician who turns stones into bread. He isn't like Superman, leaping from high buildings to make a spectacular soft landing. And when I wasn't completely cured and continued to have episodes of illness, this aspect of God was not a theory "out there". It is a very present reality with which I have to live. God is able to cure me – I know that. I have asked, and keep doing so because I want him to. And he hasn't.

At least, not yet . . .

I was once told very clearly, many years ago, "You must

thank God because he has already healed you." I had just been prayed for by a man who was well known by Christians around the world for the powerful gift of healing. Four of us had gone to Matlock, to see and hear him, and possibly to seek ministry through the laying-on of hands.

I hesitated about going. I knew, partly, that I would be going for the wrong reasons – I was intrigued to see this man and to witness some of the famous signs and wonders associated with his ministry. "But then," I consoled myself, "while Jesus was on earth, people like Zacchaeus often went to observe Jesus out of curiosity before they could trust him. If Jesus accepted their mixed motives, I'm sure God will accept me if I draw near to him, for whatever initial reason I go."

But this was only a small part of my hesitancy. There was much more than that, something which went much deeper. The trouble was, I knew what had gone before. I was almost embarrassed to recall just how often I had been forward at healing services. I had had the laying-on of hands so many times, by so many people. I had been prayed over and even anointed with oil by several men of God, including (for what it was worth) two wonderful bishops. Was it right for me to go yet again? Was I seeking something magical in this man? Because if so, was I not in danger of "worshipping" the man, rather than God himself? If it had been God I was seeking, was he not the same God, equally able to hear me and heal me, whoever laid hands on me?

Did I need to go again to ask for healing? Had God not heard me the first time? By asking for the same thing each time, was I actually evading God's response? I had an uncomfortable inkling that maybe he could have been trying hard to give me an answer, that he had some purpose in withholding physical healing.

So, I asked myself, if I went that evening, wasn't I just

trying yet another key in the lock? As if healing were like a gift in a locked cupboard, available only to those who had the right key? That contradicts the very nature of God. He does not withhold something good, just because we do not pray in the "right" way with the "right" words. After all, Jesus had despised the Pharisee's "right" form of prayer and had honoured the genuineness of the simple, humble prayer: "Lord, have mercy on me, a sinner!"

I laid aside all these questions, and more. I was persuaded to go. I felt pretty desperate: I wanted to be completely free of pain. Physical pain lingered on even though the crisis in 1980 was over and I had returned to work. Psychologically I was still in pain, too, fighting against the haunting memories that accompanied the physical symptoms I had had to endure. And emotionally, I struggled to resume my enthusiastic work as a midwife after my own hysterectomy. I had chosen to do so; I wanted to overcome; I was determined not to be defeated by it – but it was still a struggle, still a form of pain.

"Just think what you might be missing," said Alastair and Alison as they urged me to accompany them to Matlock. "Swallow your pride and come on."

The idea that it might be sheer pride which was stopping me from drawing near to God was the final straw. Dragging Matthew along with us, we jumped into the car all together.

Thus it was that, by the end of the evening, I came away asking myself what that man had meant, telling me to thank God that he had "already healed" me – because it sounded as if he was telling me to have more faith than I had. It is only after years of pondering, ruthlessly questioning myself and others – asking even God himself! – that I can articulate anything of how mistaken I know such an idea to have been.

At first my searching for an answer seemed completely

fruitless. The first glimpse I had of the impact of that man's philosophy came much later when Matthew began his ministry as a curate in Beverley. During our four years there, I came to know a lively girl named Carol. She was a teacher who was full of character and laughter. At 25 years old she was only a little younger than myself. Then, soon after we first met, she was diagnosed as having multiple sclerosis.

Carol was shattered. Such a diagnosis was to affect her whole way of living and she asked some heart-searching questions. Suddenly she and I had a lot in common. Very early in our friendship our conversations were deep and brutally honest.

One evening we sat together at a church meeting. I noticed that Carol lacked her usual sparkle and her eyes seemed distant and sad.

"How are you?" I asked, but not until I was putting my coat on, ready to leave.

"Fine, thanks."

I knew that answer very well. I had used it countless times myself.

"Rubbish!" I retorted, but with a smile. Carol looked up at me and broke into laughter at herself. She enjoyed being teased sometimes, as a normal person is, rather than constantly being pitied about her health. Her face softened with relief that she had been understood a little without her needing to go through the wearisome task of explaining her inner turmoil to me.

"It is rubbish, I know," she said at last. "Actually, Jane, I've wanted so much to talk to you. I've tried writing to you several times, but each time the letter has ended up in the waste-paper basket."

I sat down again beside her. I did not mind if we were the last people to leave the meeting – Carol needed to talk. I knew how hard I had found it to pull down my cheerful façade of saying I was "fine, thanks", and that, if I dared to do so, I wouldn't want to be ignored. Similarly for Carol now. This was the first time she had begun to let go with me and I did not want to let her down.

"Is it the MS itself which is getting you down?" I asked.

Carol shook her head. "Well, partly, I suppose. The symptoms are getting worse. I can't see properly now: everything has a double image, so I keep crashing into doors or walls, thinking that they are in a different place from where they are. And I'm also having "accidents" sometimes and I have to wear pads; but waterproof pants make a rustling noise, which is awful. Not the sort of thing to help one to make friends quickly! I get the most amazing looks from some folks, you know."

I sensed that underneath her apparent light-heartedness, Carol was quite afraid and distressed. There was nothing I could say to "help". I could offer no solution, no answer. Just, "I'm sorry". At least she knew I meant it.

Carol ventured to trust me a little further. "The thing is, while I'm acquiring these extra problems related to the MS, everyone around me – the people I love and trust – they seem to be convinced that I will be healed, and soon. I feel I'm under immense pressure."

"Pressure from their expectations, you mean?"

"Mmmm. Almost unbearable at times . . . " Carol looked away pensively before continuing. "Don't get me wrong – it would be lovely and I would be an idiot not to ask God for healing and expect it."

Carol and I had both witnessed recently the quiet miracle in our church of David, whose crippling arthritis had been healed when he was 22. Neither of us had any doubts that God does heal today. Yet Carol's experience in her suffering was different. She explained, "For example, last time I was at a healing service it was particularly difficult for me. I felt everyone in the room was expecting me to be healed, and if I wasn't then the fault could only be mine."

"How can people say that?" I bristled quite angrily at how swiftly other people can make their comments like grand pronouncements, and then they walk away forgetting everything, while the person suffering is left alone and often feeling attacked or judged.

My question was rhetorical but Carol answered nevertheless. "Oh, Jane, you know perfectly well how their argument goes. They say that God wants to heal, he wants his children to be healthy, and we have only to ask."

"Yes, I've had all that said to me," I replied. My mind went straight back to that meeting in Matlock when I had been told to thank God that he had "already healed" me. I was almost tired of hearing it.

"Quite honestly," said Carol, "I often get the feeling that it's easier for people to say that than to go a bit deeper. They can remain untouched by the pain of long-term suffering if they give a quick solution to it."

I nodded in silent agreement.

"But how do you cope, Jane, with people who try to help like this? I mean, Jesus did say, 'Ask and you shall receive'. So does that mean that these other people are right, and I just lack faith? Oh, Jane, I'm so confused."

I thought for a moment. It perturbed me to see that Carol had been upset, especially by those who intended to help, but whose care somehow became entangled or confused. I hardly knew where to start to respond to Carol. There was no simple answer.

I began gently. "Well, it didn't take long for me to realize that it isn't always as simple as some people suggest. If, as you say, we 'only have to ask', then without a doubt I would have been healed a long time ago. But I wasn't."

Carol answered quickly, "No, so we have to have faith, don't we? People say that it's my lack of faith that's stopping me from being healed."

I felt my frustration rising. I found it very hard to remain patient when people gave such a glib explanation.

"How much faith do they think you need?" I asked hotly. "Because if you look in the Bible, Jesus said all you need is faith the size of a grain of mustard seed. That's enough to move a mountain. Some Christians can make you feel utterly condemned if your faith isn't the size of a melon! But that's other people, not God. A mustard seed is enough for God. Have you got that much faith?"

Carol giggled. "Yes, I have!" She seemed pleased to have some assurance that she was not so completely feeble a Christian as she had been caused to feel, at least not on that score.

"In any case," I continued, "people who say your healing depends on you having enough faith should read Hebrews. In among the long list of heroes who are examples of those with faith, there's a little verse . . . " I fumbled to find the end of Hebrews, chapter 11. "It says, 'These were all commended for their faith, yet none of them received what had been promised. God had planned something better . . . '" I looked at Carol, whose forehead was puckering.

"What on earth does that mean?" she asked.

"It means that if we fail to receive what God has promised (like healing), we can take heart. We can be sure he has something better for us. Pressing on without receiving is actually commended! According to the person who wrote Hebrews, that is an evidence of faith."

Carol sighed ruefully. "Oh, it would be nice if things were that way round."

"I think it is that way round – when God chooses for it to be." I became very quiet before adding, "I want to hold on to that hope."

After a moment my voice became a little harder. "Anyway, if they are so impressed about the need for faith, you should remind them about Jairus' daughter, or the centurion's servant. It was the faith of the friends, and not the sufferer's faith, which Jesus congratulated. So maybe you can suggest they have more faith on your behalf, seeing as Jesus said that was so important!"

Carol was obviously too bowed under the pressure of her friends to share my laughter about that little detail. Still very puzzled, she told me soberly, "They tell me adamantly that I will be fully fit very soon." Her forehead puckered into a frown that expressed how deeply she needed to be received by her friends with simple compassion, not confused by dubious platitudes.

My cheeks flushed as I thought how people sometimes manage to avoid facing up to suffering. How much easier it was to say that Carol would be healed, than to bear the thought that she might not be. She was so bright and vivacious – how could God let her become crippled?

I burst out, "How can they be adamant? Have they asked God if that is his promise for you? Do they truly know the mind of Christ? Usually those who genuinely do have his mind are humble, not 'adamant'. Have they given time to listen to God – specifically about you and your MS? How, exactly, did it come to them that this is God's will for you?"

I could have gone on, but the glint in Carol's eye helped to stem the flow of my indignation. However, I meant every word I had said.

"You often talk about seeking God's will," Carol prompted me, her gentle tone calming after my strong outburst.

"Yes, I do." I agreed. "It's something that I learned a lot about while staying at a convent. I saw that, for the nuns there, prayer is not telling God what you want, but opening yourself to what he wants in you. For me, that takes much more faith. It means spending time silently seeking his will. I think that the only time when, as your adamant friends say, we 'just have to ask' for healing is when the Holy Spirit has told us of God's will for a particular person."

Carol nodded thoughtfully. "But according to them, I'm

not the one to know God's will. You see, you've just reminded me. They say that my lack of faith makes a wall between me and my MS, and God and his healing."

I sighed at the effect of such advice on someone like Carol whose suffering made her so vulnerable to their opinions.

"You have been confused, haven't you?" As I reached out to touch Carol's arm, trying to convey my care, her eyes moistened. I so much wanted to comfort her, to assure her of how welcomingly God accepted her, even though others had brought her disappointment, seeming only to find faults in her or her faith.

I gave Carol's arm a gentle stroke, wanting to communicate the concern and tenderness I felt, but feeling pretty impotent. "No words or arguments can help when anyone's feeling as you are now," I said. "Only you and God know if there's a wall between you. Don't rely on me or on anybody else. Just trust your own relationship with God. When you go home, do you think you could find the peaceful place where you know he is, in your own heart?"

Her nod gave me permission to say a little more, though I was wary of giving her advice. "Maybe you could try to look at him and be aware of him looking at you. You will know if there is a wall between you. And if there isn't, take courage, Carol, not to let others make you feel guilty."

Carol sniffed back her tears. "Yes, that will help," she agreed readily, reaching round for her coat.

We walked towards the door and I thought out loud, "The old devil would be thrilled if he could get at you. He knows it's hard for you to reject what loved ones say. Sometimes, though, we must do that. I think the hardest bit is recognizing when it's such a time."

I went home in a pensive mood. That night it was hard to sleep. It was all very well for me to have talked to Carol as I had, but I remembered times when I had felt hurt, as she was now. Deeply hurt. I thought of how often I had found myself alone after visitors had left me, feeling as if it was all my own fault that I was not better. People may have meant kindly, but I'm sure they could not have realized how devastated I was by some of their advice.

The sorts of things they said went round and round my head as I tossed and turned in bed. "I've just been reading Matthew's gospel where Jesus says, 'Ask and you will receive.'" (How often I had heard that!) "Well, presumably, Jane, you can't have asked him properly?"

Not asked – pleaded! Besought. Hammered at his door. Wept. Cried out. Thrown myself at his feet. If God hadn't heard me, he was not the God whom I knew I could trust.

I remembered, with some measure of shame, one time when a man I shall call Mike had got in touch with me. We did not know each other well but he had heard about my illness at his church. He had been concerned and, as well as praying for me, he had also wanted to do something tangible to help. He had decided to visit me at home.

I had found the time with him very tense. Not one of his "helpful" suggestions was new to me, though he was clearly very enthusiastic about each one. Unfortunately (and this was where I felt somewhat ashamed as I recalled the scene) I did not have the emotional energy to be anything more than blunt in my replies. I shudder, now, as I look back at my arrogance.

"You should pray in Jesus' name."

"I always do."

"Why don't you call together the elders of the church for laying-on of hands – as in James 5?"

"I have. Lots of times."

"You should be anointed with oil."

"I have been."

"You need to find out if there's something in your past which is preventing you from being healed."

"I went to a Christian psychiatrist, with Matthew, to pursue that one. After two sessions, she described me as pretty well balanced with fairly usual sorts of hang-ups. She stopped because, she said, there was nothing abnormally wrong to cause sickness."

I am ashamed at how quickly I dismissed that subject, in one sweep. I had so much yet to learn, so far still to journey along my pathway. However, one reason for my quick answers is that I was rebelling against his attitude. He seemed to have judged me before he'd even met me. He spoke as if he had all the answers. The longer I live, the fewer answers I have. They have been replaced by questions and, thank God, a growing ability to respect paradox.

"You ought to go to such-and-such a man. He has a healing ministry."

"I went last year."

I wanted Mike to stop giving me a formula. I wanted him to see that not one thing had "worked"; I had done all the things he was suggesting and was still left in pain. I wanted him to stop and think. I was trying – ungraciously, I know – to make him realize that, although his mind was fixed on physical healing, there was an alternative to the way in which he was talking.

Finally, he had sighed, exhausted. "Then you must have been healed. You should thank God."

There was that phrase again! At that point in the conversation my hands were clutching a hot-water bottle under the duvet, as I tried to find something to soothe the pain searing through me. There used to be a time when I would have wondered if it were just my imagination that I was still in great pain when someone was telling me that I had been healed. But not this time.

I felt so strongly that Mike was barging in on a delicate subject, that I was reluctant to give him my time. Yet in the end God's graciousness prevailed and I did try to explain a little.

"My first reaction to this pain continuing on and on was to think, like you now, that praying for healing was something I must do correctly in order to get what I wanted," I told him. "When I clearly 'failed', I was caused to start thinking in a completely different way about prayer."

Mike looked at me suspiciously. I prayed silently, asking God to help me to stay patient and be honest.

"When I pray now, I concentrate very much less on what I am actually asking for. I am sure he wants us to seek more of who he is. Only then can he reveal how to pray about specific things."

Mike's face furrowed. I was risking a lot by trying to explain myself. I was laying myself open to accusations or criticism about my own spiritual journey. Could he understand me, I wondered? My prayer life was a personal matter and I knew that I should not mind what anyone else thought about it, but even so I felt open to Mike's judgement.

I tried to explain. "One of the nuns at a convent I once visited put it much better than I can. She said, 'Prayer is not an easy way of getting God to do things for you, but a difficult way of allowing him to do things in you.'"

"Isn't that just playing with words?" asked Mike suspiciously. "What's the difference?"

"The difference is in the answer we seek. The 'answer' to prayer is not in receiving a gift, but in meeting the Giver."

I realized that I was trying to condense into one conversation all that God had been teaching me over many years. Healing was an enormous subject, of which prayer was only one part. I tried to put very simply what was uppermost in my mind.

"I believe God wants the best for us, always."

"Right."

"My idea of the best is healing."

"Right."

"But God has withheld that, despite my asking for it in

all the ways I have told you. Now, I could blame myself for lacking faith, or somehow not asking in the right way. But I know that I have asked in every way I can, and not alone but with the support of many faithful Christians."

"Yes?" Mike was not quite sure he could trust me. Again I uttered a quick prayer asking God to help me to be more concerned about speaking truthfully than about what Mike thought of me.

"Or I could blame God, saying either that he has not heard me or that he is mean, withholding something good. But I cannot do either of those things, because deep down I trust him. I just know that he does not delight in making his children suffer."

I had to show that I was still genuinely looking to God, despite not sharing Mike's view. I had sounded so negative when he had first arrived that he might have thought I was dismissive of God. He would have been so wrong. I know God always wants to do more for me and in me than ever I can imagine.

"So it must be something else." I paused. I did not want to say what was so important to me if Mike was not listening properly.

"What?" he asked, interested. It had never occurred to him that, unlike us, God himself might actually have wanted something other than physical healing for me at that point in time.

"I can only conclude that he has not healed me physically because he has something better for me. I said before, my idea of the best is feeling well. But at the moment anyway, it seems that that's not God's idea of the best. He does say, 'My ways are not your ways'. Although this dreadful pain is not my way, or the way I would choose, it seems obvious that it's his."

"That's very harsh, isn't it?" At least Mike was thinking about what I had said.

"No," I replied. "It seems harsh and it feels harsh; but I stake everything on my faith that God is not harsh. And I am not alone in believing that, contrary to our assumptions, God is doing something better and deeper."

"Who else says that?"

Now that we were conversing, instead of fighting, there was time to tell Mike a story by way of reply, to illustrate my meaning. Matthew's mother had received a letter from a friend of hers who, although he did not know me, had been praying for me. As he had prayed, a picture had formed in his mind, one he felt impelled to share and to pass on to me. He wrote:

> I could see the face of Christ, who was looking upon Jane in her suffering. I had been surprised that, instead of encountering pain and confusion, there had been great joy and light. Jesus was looking with desire and love upon what he saw forming and coming out of the pain. Though he was mindful of the pain, the Lord took delight in the very thing which I found hard.

I told Mike how much that letter encouraged me. It led me to see my suffering more from God's point of view. It really helped me to feel some of his joy.

"How could God ever want pain?" Mike was very puzzled.

"Oh, I don't know." I sighed. "I don't have all the answers. I cannot explain God. I can only tell you as much as I do know so far. And encouragements such as that letter confirm to me that it isn't folly to trust God to be doing something good, even though it feels totally grim."

"It's very different from my starting-point," Mike said.

"But Mike," I said eagerly, because at least he was listening now. "Every time I have gone forward for laying-on of hands for healing, the physical pain has become worse rather than better. *But* alongside this I have been given a huge injection of closeness to the Lord. It's as if God takes me, lifts me up and reassures me that he is doing with me just what he wills."

"And do you really thank him for that?" Mike was pressing me very hard for sincere answers.

I paused. "Sometimes." I hugged the hot-water bottle more closely to myself. "I wish I could honestly say always. If I had been healed physically, I'd have leapt up and said, 'Thank you, Lord!' Well, just because I can't see the areas where he is healing, shouldn't I still be thanking him? I suspect that his healing in me is much deeper than anything physical. Because there's one thing of which I am very sure. Healing is not the same as cure."

We were both thoughtful. At last Mike arrived at a conclusion from what he had gained through our conversation.

"You reminded me of the story of the ten lepers," he said. "They were all healed, physically. Yet nine out of ten of them went off without speaking to Jesus again: not even to thank him. It seems to me that it's quite a miracle that you've at least kept coming to him."

I lay back on the pillows and smiled. I no longer felt accused. At last Mike and I were communicating, rather than fighting against one another. He had understood – at least a little. He had recognized that suffering could be a vehicle for faithfulness and trust in God; he saw that it was not necessarily proof of faithlessness. The relief of that was very valuable.

What I had been trying to share with him was the acceptance to which God had brought me after the terrible crisis at Tina's college flat. I had only talked about it so directly once before, and that was to Graham, Matthew's tutor. As I sat in Colin's house, waiting to go back into hospital and not knowing how long I would even live, Graham had asked me, "Do you feel God is ignoring your pain, or that he is letting things get out of hand?"

"No." I was sure of my answer despite the desperate anguish I felt. "No, I don't. I don't like what he's doing. But I've put myself in his hands and asked him to do the best for me. I can trust his wisdom. While I loathe the pain itself, I refuse to be tempted to stop trusting him. He knows best. Having asked him to do his will I can only trust him that what's happening to me now is his will."

"How are you so sure?" Graham had asked me.

I replied honestly. "Because God is in it. It's accompanied by such peace, such an assurance of him with me that I know this can't all be his mistake."

This was my conviction. To abandon myself completely into his hands, no matter what pain that caused in me. To follow him obediently – even to the furnace for him to purify me; to the garden for him to prune me, cutting back good growth and making room for even more; to the threshing-mill for him to thrash out the wheat from the chaff. This was healing.

At the healing service in Matlock, the man crouching over me had said, "You must thank God that he has already healed you." Maybe he was right. But I have found that, whenever I think of the word "healed" to mean "cured", I diminish what God has been doing. God's healing is much broader, deeper and more creative than any of my short-sighted, pain-free solutions.

As I followed my pathway, I came to appreciate that healing was something to do with being taken more deeply into God. That is of immeasurable value. To lose sight of that is to lose sight of God himself. Whenever I have allowed myself to fall into that trap, I have been cast into the desolation of crying, "My God, my God, why have you forsaken me?"

CHAPTER SEVEN

"WHY HAVE YOU FORSAKEN ME?"

Psalm 22:1

Resuming normal life after a long period of illness has always signified far more to me than merely the end of convalescence. My return to work in September 1980 brought to a head my difficulty in living out a peaceful equilibrium between the enormous contrasts within me. I felt I was juggling because I was constantly trying to balance the story of my pain with that of my successes.

As soon as I was back, I was confronted again by my "successes" in midwifery. One hesitates to write boastfully about oneself, but it was evident that I was popular among the patients and sought after by the consultants. Patients did not hide their disappointment that they had not had me to look after them throughout their pregnancy and labour, and many of the staff shared openly their relief that "at last things will be done properly again!"

It did not stop there. While I had been off work, a simple audio-visual programme which I had compiled had begun to be used in other hospitals around Britain. It was being given enthusiastic praise from other midwives, and before long I was flown down to London to receive a national award. During that trip I was commissioned to create five new films which were to be distributed around the world.

I was positively exhilarated. I had known utter broken-ness in my pain, but now I was tasting again great fulfil-ment. Soon I was lecturing to other health professionals, first in Britain and then internationally, as far afield as Australia. Once again, I was able to enjoy the glow of achievement and satisfaction, perhaps all the more so because now I felt I saw it in a healthier perspective.

When others looked at me, they saw a strong person. I typified the character of the department, well known for combining efficiency with good fun. Most of the time, I myself felt confident, even elated, that things were going so well.

And yet . . . and yet. What of the pain? How did that find its place in the life of one for whom everything else was going so well in so many areas? Not least among all the happy-making events surrounding us was the news in 1982 that we would expect our first baby by adoption. Should we therefore have seen things as many of our friends did, that all this apparent "blessing" was some form of compen-sation from on high for all we'd suffered? Was the adoption of our son and, three years later, our daughter, the joyful beginning of what has continued to be a most wonderful gift to us of a family – was that like the icing on the cake for us, to make up for everything?

If this is so, then my emotions have not been guided by reason, for there have been times – there still are – when it seems that no amount of good things can ever counterbal-ance the utter brokenness within. For years I continued to feel weak, vulnerable, torn apart either by the pain or by the memories of it. My heart had been broken and I didn't know if life would ever be the same again.

Often my longing took the form of a subconscious craving for quiet, unspoken understanding and comfort rather than a specific need I could describe. At such times I felt completely unable to ask for help; it took me years even to have any idea of how one could even begin to learn to do so. Those who saw only the fruitfulness of my life did not realize my unspoken needs. And so, all too easily, times have developed when I have felt forsaken both by others and, more distressingly, by God himself.

I remember one such occasion very well. Lying down to rest alone one afternoon, I was suddenly aware of the hurt, confusion and loneliness that filled my mind and soul.

I had been invited to lecture at another World Congress. After two years out of clinical work since the birth of our son, I knew I would benefit not only from the three days' academic stimulation and challenge but also from the luxury of being looked after in an expensive hotel.

Outwardly, everything went very well. During my first lecture on the first day, I had felt inspired, and the hundreds of nurses and health visitors listening had responded enthusiastically. At one point they had burst into spontaneous applause and laughter, quickly melting my nervousness in front of so many professionals. That was sufficient boost to my confidence for me to be looking forward to the workshop I was to lead the following morning.

Back in my plush hotel room that evening, I was revelling in the comfort of it all. A phone call home had given me the opportunity for a lovely chat, not only with Matthew but also with a very happy two-year-old. "Did you see Princess Anne, Mummy?" was all he had wanted to know. I chuckled to myself as I lay soaking in a bath full of bubbles later that evening. As I committed the day to God, I remembered a verse in Joel which someone had once thought applied very specially to me: "I will restore the years which the locusts have eaten."

I had had years of being stripped of everything through my pain. But I had had much restored: my fulfilment now, my career, even a family against all the odds. I thanked God for his many blessings, climbed into bed, and drifted off into a very contented sleep.

But the next morning I was suddenly plunged into distress. I had taken a long time to wake up completely. As often happens, the abdominal discomfort that had become "normal" for me had been incorporated into my dreams.

This time, my dream took me back to the time when I was first ill, in Edinburgh. Half awake, half dreaming, I felt as I had then – too limp to move my heavy body for myself. I was aware of my heavy breathing, of my body position stretched out completely limp on the bed. In the dream, I relived the time when my breathing had been laboured because of illness, and my limp body had been placed in a similar stretched-out position by the nurses.

It was only the faintest stirring in me which strove towards consciousness: this time because I was still mostly asleep. In Edinburgh I had been unable to waken myself fully because of the severity of the peritonitis. Overwhelmed by the pain of the whole situation, I had lain completely passive – all except for this one tiny stirring in me which struggled, even against my own will, to fight its way to life.

Although that anguish was only a memory, it was so vivid that I felt as if the situation were actually repeating itself in reality. But in Edinburgh, there had been consolation. I had been comforted then, in a visit from one of my nursing tutors, Elaine. She had drawn alongside and had actually *shown* her compassion to me, even though at the time I was too weak to respond. Her caring hand had gently held my forearm. It was as simple as that.

As I woke from my dream, I longed for a gentle caress. I was reliving the scene, but without her caring touch. Without it, I felt bereft. I wanted so much to be able to be comforted *in my passivity*. I wanted to see someone like Elaine, not only beside me physically but "with" me in understanding, as she had been. In my sleepiness the pain was vivid and alive; but in my semi-consciousness I also knew no one was there to help or soothe. I felt forsaken.

For as long as I could, I kept my eyes tightly closed, at least trying to envisage Elaine's care, and grasp it to meet my present need. If I could not be comforted as I would have liked, then at least I would try to imagine it.

Eventually the dream faded until I could no longer hold on to it. It was but a memory. The vision of someone caring for me was just a fancy. I struggled to put it out of my mind.

All of that day, I felt very fragile. The pain was "only" in my mind, I knew, yet I could not shrug it off. It was as if I was still enduring it, and therefore I still needed to be comforted with the sort of comfort I had once experienced. As always after a dream such as that, I was back to forcing myself to do everything. Not least, I had a workshop to lead.

And of course, people saw no need to comfort me. They saw the competent image I presented: no one saw the pain within. In one sense I wanted it like that: I certainly did not want to be pitied or made a fuss of. Deep down, however, I felt very alone. I could hear the cry of my broken heart.

Occasionally during the day, I found myself close to tears, bearing so vividly what I wanted to keep in the past.

"Don't be silly," I chided myself. "You're not ill now; you don't need comforting."

But pain is a peculiar thing. Its emotional effects last far longer than clock-time; or it can re-visit a person long after its physical cause has passed. It does not go away to order, with reasoning or bargaining. It is a silent guest that comes and goes as it pleases.

I tried to pray. "Lord, these memories of pain are troubling me. I feel so confused and unsettled. I yearn to be comforted. You understand better than anyone else; you know more about me than I do about myself. You be the one to hold me and please, please! Let me *feel* you. Speak reassuringly to me. Let me see your eyes: I know they are full of compassion. Let me feel the tenderness of your love which I know is there."

But he did not. It was as if he were not there. As if he had withdrawn. Physically, emotionally, even spiritually, I felt utterly forsaken.

None of the events of the day could console me in the emptiness I felt. This was something at the core of my being: a child unable to see her beloved Father. It was God himself who seemed distant. No external blessing could ever compensate for that. I was weighed down in spirit, as if under a cloud. Outward achievements only served to lure me into self-satisfaction, which dragged me even further away from the childlike place where I wanted to be. I wanted to feel myself to be lifted on to God's knee where I would be close to his heart; I could nestle into his breast and hear his soft heartbeat.

By the time my workshop was over, I was exhausted. As soon as the mêlée of people asking me questions had left, I slipped back to my room in the adjoining hotel. I had been forcing myself so much, I had to rest. With relief I drank in the soothing quietness of the beautiful hotel room, so pleasant after the tiring buzz of noise and constant chatter in the conference. I locked the door firmly and flopped on to the bed.

Once again, as soon as I closed my eyes I was straight back to that scene in Edinburgh. I could not push out of my mind that memory of my profound illness and weakness. I recalled how I had been unable even to swallow. I could almost feel again the saliva dribbling from my mouth, down the side of my cheek and on to the shoulder of that unfeminine hospital gown draped around me.

I was disturbed by all this, distressed to relive such weakness and pain. Yet, in a way, I wanted to relive it if – if

– I could reach back to the place where I could remember Elaine's care once again. I felt I could feast on that recollection until I had had my fill.

I was so torn! I must have known that, in the end, I would never have my fill. I was mistaken to look backwards for comfort I needed in the present. I yet had to learn that lesson. At the time, I was so overwhelmed by that aching void within, I was consumed by my desperation to fill it. To try to grasp past consolation actually made things worse because I became so bowed down by the memory of the pain that I merely felt increasingly vulnerable, isolated, and far from any comfort.

"Help me, Lord!" I moaned. "Please help me." I buried my head in the soft pillow.

There was no "answer". No response. I felt no different. God was silent. The only relief was to allow the tears to flow at last, after holding them back all morning at the conference.

I wanted to look towards God for help and I felt let down by him. I was in trouble; this was one of the times when I needed him most of all. And this was the very time he had chosen to hide his face from me.

Hardly daring to speak resentfully towards him, instead I fumbled for my Bible and allowed the psalmist to express my own bewildered questions:

> Why are you so far away, O Lord?
> Why do you hide yourself when we are in trouble?
> (Psalm 10:1, GNB)

> How much longer will you forget me, Lord?
> For ever? . . .
> How long will sorrow fill my heart day and night?
> (Psalm 13:1–2, GNB)

Strangely, I had no doubt in my mind that God was with me, even though I could not feel him. I can only think that he had given me this faith; certainly I could take no credit for it myself. The frustration was knowing that he, my Father, was there . . . but in darkness.

God was not visible. He was not where I wanted him. He had promised to be with me, always, but I could not feel him. I knew off by heart a verse in Psalm 77: "Your path led through the sea, your way through the mighty waters, though your footprints were not seen." That described my own pathway through this pain.

One reassurance to me, once I was a little calmer, was that I knew I was not the only person to experience spiritual "darkness", as it is called. I had read a little of the spiritual masters and I found their experience consoling because they seemed not to be surprised at this phenomenon. They described it to be a special calling, to know him in darkness. Sister Rachel-Mary had been very encouraging to me, too. She was one of the rare people who truly seemed to identify with this forsakenness, and therefore I could respect the wisdom of what she had once written to me:

> If you are going to go deeper into a "knowledge" of God you will be drawn into the wilderness to teach you the real meaning of faith. God does withdraw the "knowledge" of his presence in the realm of feelings, and we have to learn that Love is of the will and not the emotions, so that we will "love him though he slay" us.
>
> It is just the going on, going on, with no feedback ourselves. As and when he wills, God will give you a glimpse of the sun. There will be a break in the clouds – just enough to keep you going on again in the dark.
>
> It may surprise you, but for myself this darkness has been the norm all the time in community until about a year ago! It all sounds challenging and good etc., and so it is; but it feels like hell (and so, I suppose, it is!).

However, there was one danger. I was aware that, while God could withdraw himself from the realm of our feelings in order to deepen our faith, it is also true that his enemy the devil could use the same circumstance to try to turn us away from God. So, even in my pitiful state, I said aloud with as much authority as I could muster, "And if you, devil, have anything to do with this, then you can just go away! You have no business to taunt me. I am a child of God, my Father. In the name of the Lord Jesus, just go away!"

After that, I knew I must try to distract my wandering thoughts. My will-power was stretched to the limits, so alluring was the temptation to indulge in flights of imagination. I turned towards the shining metal panel beside my bed and switched on the radio. The sound of pop music was just fading. A disc-jockey began talking about the birth of a self-help group. He described how a couple had lost their baby. The doctors and nurses had been very kind, but all too soon after the death, formal help had diminished. Friends began to stop talking about the couple's grief. Every form of help they had first received gradually stopped. Yet their need for care and comfort had continued.

They could have been describing me!

Next, the couple on the radio spoke up for themselves. "No amount of sympathy can stop you having to go through things," they said. "We had an aching void which was just not filled. We formed our group to help ourselves and others in a similar unhappy position."

Sloppy music was playing in the background. At the end of their "moving story", as he put it, the disc-jockey added his own comments.

"Oh, you admire the courage of that couple, don't you, when you hear how they surmounted that kind of unhappiness?" he said sentimentally in his deep voice. Then the jangle of the next record boomed out and coaxed us all into a carefree mood once again.

But they had had no choice! My heart screamed in silence.

I groaned into my pillow. I didn't find their story either romantic or heroic, as he had described it. He was blind to the other half of the story. He saw where they had been brave, but that was undoubtedly only one part of them. There would be another part that would be crying out with the pain of their loss and their grief – just as surely as I was crying out with mine as I listened.

He had made that couple's courage sound so glorious, but it would not have felt like that to them. They had probably felt totally unable to surmount their pain but how can people express their inability to do so? There is no option, no way out. Pain simply takes its victim over. It governs every move, almost like a machine which has been wound up and cannot stop until it has run its course. Under its influence and direction, I had often felt as if I just had to act out the awful mechanics of living in pain.

The couple might enjoy admiration for a while, but no amount of admiration counterbalances the heart's deep pain. What counts is a sense of being profoundly and tenderly understood and cared for.

The attractive aspect of my dream and the memory of Elaine's visit to me in Edinburgh was that I had been comforted in my weakness. I had not had to fight to prove to her that I was brave. What I treasured in my memory was not her admiration, but her compassion. She had comforted me in my passivity even before I had known that she was beside me. For once I had been "caught" – unable to strive to show my courage. It was an unusual situation for me. I do not normally lie back and enjoy being comforted in weakness. To do so would feel like an indulgence in wallowing.

I turned over in bed, becoming drowsy with the radio's

soft music. At last I slept, managing some escape, at least, from the heaviness of some of my thoughts.

I awoke gently the next time, and tried to refresh myself for the conference once again. Standing under the shower in the elaborate hotel bathroom, I glanced up. The huge tinted mirror along one wall reflected my figure. The scar right down my abdomen seemed to glare back at me, prominent and red. At that moment I hated it, or rather, what it represented. I did not want to look. Quickly I wrapped my warm towel around me and began to dress.

Was I covering up the story of my pain? Did I "cope" by hiding and suppressing what hurt? A particular phrase was ringing round in my head. So often I had heard people say, "I don't know how you cope so marvellously . . . "

They are so wrong. They take me for what I seem to be. I do not feel brave. I do not deserve admiration. Inside myself, I do not "cope marvellously". Whenever I have acute bouts of pain I have to struggle every minute, every hour, against crying out loud with tears.

Throughout the whole day at the conference, I told no one of my inner desolation. I could not. What could I have said? There was a tedious history behind the inner pain I felt; how could anyone have understood it all?

In many ways, I could see why people remarked that I coped marvellously. I usually made myself appear normal, just as I was on that day; I enjoyed doing so. But I also realized that throwing myself into life as I did prevented others from knowing my pain. If I had ever dared to share with people how I felt deep-down, they had invariably responded by saying, "Jane, I never knew."

That's it. They never really know. Pain is one's own. Others cannot know it all. Perhaps everyone is in pain, with their own pain, living in corporate isolation from one another. As the couple on the radio had said, "Others may help you cope but in the end it's you that has to go through it."

But I was a Christian, I reproached myself. God cares; he helps people through everything. How could I feel alone when he has promised to be with us, always? I have received so much, and especially I have been supported and cared for by family and friends. Was I being ungrateful by feeling alone?

I hope not. Matthew often assured me that he understood too well ever to accuse me of that. However close we were to one another, he was still not the one who had to bear what I did. That, in a way, was the awful thing he had to bear: to watch, to care, but to be unable to take the pain away.

It was a long time afterwards that I talked this through with a very dear friend, Sarah. I was again very low with yet another episode of pain. "I don't know what to say to you, Jane," she said wretchedly. She did not know the relief she brought by simply holding questions with me instead of giving answers. She too had personal struggles which she needed to talk about. She had once found it particularly hard to hold on to her faith in the goodness of God. By sharing with one another about the times when we had each reached rock-bottom, we maybe brought to one another the presence of God himself. Certainly it was something very precious.

"I feel terribly impotent, being so useless. But there's nothing I can do to help you," she said apologetically.

"You have helped," I told her with conviction. "You always make time to listen, without making me feel I'm a nuisance to you; you find some encouragement without sounding empty. You will remain someone whom I can always trust at least to try to understand."

It was true. One source of my heavy-heartedness was, sadly, those Christians who have just shrugged their shoulders and said, "Ah well, God knows best!" Their tone of voice sounded as light-hearted as that nurse back in 1980, "I heard you had your hyst.". They sounded to me as if they were dismissing any thought of things hurting more deeply than they imagined. They wanted to look on the bright side and no doubt their aim was to cheer me up by doing likewise. But I'm afraid that that attitude has me feeling even more isolated. I am unable to toss away all thought of pain and difficulties as they seem to do. That accentuates the real loneliness.

I sometimes wonder if the loneliness of pain is perhaps its most excruciating aspect. It threatens to cut one off from others: and then to feel – worst of all – that one is abandoned by God himself. However, the truth is that it is not a mere fancy but God's *promise* that he is with us always. His apparent absence has us searching for him all the more. And whenever I do glimpse his truth, when I hold on to him and know I am *held*, then I find that it might be possible to "endure with patience".

CHAPTER EIGHT

"ENDURE WITH PATIENCE"

2 Corinthians 1:6

It is now 25 years since I first developed an abscess following the original appendix operation in 1976. For those years I have yo-yo'd up and down, improving and relapsing, in and out of hospital. The time has been punctuated, but not relieved, by several major operations. And because little changed outwardly, I came to believe that God had called me to trust him in darkness, to keep holding his hand even (especially) through the pain. He wants me to endure all things with him.

Unfortunately I cannot simply disregard the pain or turn my back on suffering. It is only possible to live to the full by accepting life to the full – and that includes whatever we find very difficult. It means accepting everything, even pain and vomiting, as part of me, part of being myself. The pain I carry is not an optional extra, like a handbag that I can either forget I am carrying, or that I can lay down. No: it is integral to my life.

It is a hard path. In the wake of serious illness, tiredness can feel more like a shut-down of the body. Suddenly, unbidden, while shopping, or in the middle of an interesting exhibition, or being out at a dinner party for example, I will feel the weight of utter exhaustion. I feel wretched and my thoughts are overtaken by a longing to lie down. At last – at last! – I am beginning to learn to dare to ask to do so. I write "dare" because I have to dare to trust friends to understand and not to think of me as a sissy. That old feeling still taunts me, and here I am in my middle 40s before I'm on the road to overcoming it! But that's not my only discomfort. Inevitably, whenever I am overwhelmed by exhaustion, I remember *why* I am particularly susceptible to such tiredness and in my mind's eye I can be hurtled straight back to being thrust into an ambulance, into hospital, on a trolley or surrounded by the silent tension of intensive care.

I still need to rest – sleep – for two hours every afternoon. Even then, occasionally tiredness consumes days or sometimes whole weeks at a time, sapping me of vivacity and humour and life in its fullness. Often I am too tired to read, too weary even to knit or embroider, because the weight of my arms feels too great. When I first waken from sleep I do not feel rested. I am still aware of the energy involved in lifting my head up to turn towards the clock. When the pain has been bad for some time, even breathing is tiring, such that I notice the effort in moving my chest or in opening my nostrils. Holding my arms and body together in its very existence feels too much. I often feel just too weary.

I wonder how long I will keep going in this sort of state, but somehow I am still here. I have to put conscious effort into making my muscles hold me standing upright. At times like these, people must wonder why I don't concentrate well on a conversation! I feel as if I am on autopilot, forcing myself to walk, throwing one step after another, hoping I will not fall. Except, sometimes, I wish that I could fall, and let myself go completely, so that I could be free of feeling the weight of my body alive.

Time drags. I try to stop myself looking at the clock. But

then suddenly I realize that more time has passed than I had guessed, and that seems a real blessing. I look forward to this painful phase of life being over.

But as "this phase" of life goes on and on, I realize that pain is an integral part of my very living. I cannot wait for life to pass, so I have to get down to living without watching the minutes ticking by. I cannot "leave my pain at the cross", as some Christians would urge, because I feel like the boy in a wheelchair in the haunting poster that says, "He can't walk away from this". Neither can I walk away without my pain. Instead, I have to throw myself into making the most of my living in pain.

It's one thing to cope with the actual physical endurance of my tummy being sore. That is at least contained in one place. But I loathe to see the effect rippling out to others, especially Matthew. It changes our relationship and sometimes I feel bitter that pain could succeed in its assaults upon something so precious.

As always, it's the silly little things which precipitate inordinately heated responses. Instead of our giving one another strength to pull together against the suffering, all too easily things can somehow be turned around until we seem to be pulling against one another.

Not only do I reach the end of my tether with my own pain, but also Matthew does with his. It's as if he can last for so long watching me, feeling sympathetic and supportive towards me, before he reaches the limits of his unselfishness. Suddenly he will become aware of the cost to him and he will resent it. Not me: it. But I, watching him, feel that I am to blame. The pain is mine: could I not cope better so that he does not have to suffer as well?

I remember one particular day in the midst of a week in which I was struggling simply to keep going. I was forcing myself round the house trying to do the basic chores. I had thought I was doing well until, suddenly, I heard the scraping noise of the smart wooden stools being kicked roughly under the breakfast bar.

"No butter!" came a heated expletive. Matthew was peeved. He likes butter on his toast in the morning: that is one of his treats.

I cringed. I felt accused, even though he had been shouting at the situation, not at me personally. He had not known that I was just above the kitchen, slowly folding the washing from the airing cupboard. (Keep on your feet, Jane. Don't dream about lying down. You must do this first.) Mind you, he was sufficiently angry that he probably wouldn't have minded that I heard.

My thoughts scanned the past few days. Why was there no butter? How had I managed to let the old one run out without replacing it? I felt I had failed as Matthew's wife. A decent wife would ensure there was always enough butter for her husband's toast.

I remembered taking the empty butter dish over to the kitchen sink on the previous day. I must get a new packet from the freezer, I had thought wearily as I took the brush to wash it. Then, "later", I had added, thinking how far away the garage seemed at that moment. And later, of course, I had forgotten.

Now as I carried the neatly folded tea-towels down to the kitchen I wondered what to say when I saw Matthew. This was my fault. I could not really blame pain for such a small thing. I had been lazy, then I had forgotten.

Matthew was not there. He was bashing about in his study now. Up on the wall, the shopping list was pinned as usual to the notice-board. Its whole page was filled with one word sprawled across it:

"B U T T E R".

I felt very sorry for myself as I closed the drawer on my fresh supply of tea-towels. I thought of all that I had done over the past week, battling against how I had felt physically. And Matthew wasn't appreciative of what I *had* done. All he was doing this morning was shouting at what I had failed to do.

In this sense of failure, feeling overwhelmed by pain, one of the worst things I can do is to look ahead and imagine everything continuing like that for ever. To endure patiently is much harder when there seems to be no time-limit to the pain. How quickly a feeling of desperation, a sort of claustrophobia, can come. I can rapidly become down-hearted as even slight episodes trigger off the memory of the depth of anguish associated with similar pain.

The most tedious aspect of chronic pain is its relentless-ness, continuing on and on. I sometimes feel trapped by it; I am living in pain. I find myself saying, "I cannot bear this." I feel I could somehow cope if I could look forward to a day or a time when the pain will end, to console myself that I will soon feel better. Even the same afternoon can seem exhaustingly far ahead, and I think, "I cannot get through until the children are in bed. I'll surely crack up before then!" But that is looking ahead.

Instead, I am trying to learn how to look only at the present. I should say to myself, "You are bearing it, Jane", because pain is deceptive. It gives the impression that it will overwhelm for a long time. In practice, often just one day makes a huge difference. Within a few hours, unbearable pain can change and become almost bearable. And of course, it is well known that pain is affected by morale. I am only just learning to shed my shame in confessing that the most stupid little things, such as washing the dishes, can lift my morale enough to make the pain seem less intolerable.

Others can and do help. Matthew and I are frequently amazed by the sacrifices made by family and friends in order to help us, in whatever ways they choose. One day a friend, Annegret, telephoned to ask after me. I told her I was unwell again. This time, things were not so bad as to warrant admission to hospital, but I was in a lot of pain. Within two hours she had come round to the house, bringing food she had lovingly cooked for the family for the next week. She considered this to be meagre help in the face of such suffering; she would have preferred to take away my pain. Yet her visit to me was like a visit from God himself saying, "This is a sign that I care about you, including in the practicalities".

And yet, even help can have its drawbacks. People do what seems best and that is not always what might help most. On another occasion when the children were very young, two people came unannounced with four meals between them. A big treat? Yes, except that all of it had previously been frozen and required to be eaten soon. To make matters more complicated, there was already food in our fridge which had to be cooked before it went stale. So while outwardly thanking the caring friends for their thoughtful gifts, Matthew was inwardly groaning. He still had to cook; he still had to think how he could best use the food; he still had to plan which dish had to be cooked most immediately. And, by the time he closed the door on those friends, the children were bored.

The sitting-room looked uninviting and stale now. The glass-topped tables were smeared with grubby fingermarks. Shelves were cluttered with empty cups. Matthew dragged himself into the depressing scene, just in time to catch our daughter. Enjoying her new-found skill of crawling, she had just reached up for the brightly shining sugar bowl. As she grabbed clumsily for it, she knocked over a half-empty cup.

"Disgusting!" muttered Matthew under his breath, stomping heavily towards her. He lifted her exploring arms from patting the cold tea, now dripping on to the carpet, and carried her through to the kitchen to wash her. There, too, he was met with a mess. Cake tins were still left out from the folk who had brought the food. He snapped one lid closed but, before he could put it away, there was a sudden wail from the sitting-room.

The older child had become bored after enduring visitors one after another. Each had excluded him from their discussions of "important" things. At three years old he could have made his own contribution to the conversation about Mummy's sore tummy. He would have enjoyed explaining that she had had a tube put into her "bud vessel" which he thought looked like a train going along a railway line. But people had not expected him to converse, so he had not. Instead he had set up an assault course, jumping from a wooden chair on to a huge floor cushion. It had amused him for a while, until one jump when he had bumped his head on the bookshelf by mistake.

Matthew raced through. Tears flowed freely, but more out of boredom than the bump on his head. This child needed to declare that he wanted as much time with Daddy as others got. Grown-ups somehow had the knack of demanding attention immediately: when they rang the doorbell, Matthew answered it and there ensued a conversation. The children came second to the doorbell or the telephone. They were still too little to have learned how to demand time sociably from Matthew's busy life, except by a huge wail.

Matthew sat cradling his son, stroking his hair. He admired the assault course and soon they were both laughing about the bumped head. "Bumps will happen if we do dangerous things in life," they agreed. "Pain is OK when we've had fun."

Upstairs in bed, I heard it all.

"Would you like a story?" Matthew suggested. Stories were a good opportunity for a quietly intimate time together. That would entertain both children together. "Oooh!" came the enthusiastic reply, and the older one ran to choose a book.

But Matthew's voice did not hold his usual enthusiasm.

His reading was mechanical today. His mind was not with Thomas the Tank Engine. It was in the study, thinking about his work. He needed space to think. How best could he encourage those four mums to help with a new pram service in church? How were the three teenagers coping whose mother had died recently? What could he do to catch the interest of the children in tomorrow's school assembly? That was work. His work. Amusing children was not real work: not in the same, fulfilling way. How could he do justice to God in his work this week without time? Time to think? And pray?

Once the story was over, our toddler contentedly emptying a fresh box of toys, Matthew planned to snatch a few moments to think on his own. He began to gather together the empty mugs. "You just carry on while I try to tidy up a bit," he suggested to the children.

But the older one was still bored; no suggestion caught his imagination now. "May I watch television? My programme?" he asked, recognizing the distinctive set of the clock's hands at 4p.m. for the start of children's television.

Matthew was thwarted from carrying through the dishes. He turned round, frustrated from his plans and cross that a little bit more of his attention had been squeezed from him. A little bit more, and a little bit more. If it wasn't friends calling, it was the telephone, or one child or the other. And he hadn't been upstairs to see me for a while . . . me, shedding a quiet tear after hearing their earlier conversation. "Pain is OK when we've had fun . . . " they had said. What about when it prevents us having fun in the first place, I was wondering? I was glad Matthew had not come up. My tears, however quiet, would only have been yet another burden on him. He was suffering enough already.

"Well, it depends what the TV programme is," Matthew conceded reluctantly. But before Matthew had even completed his answer, the switch had been pressed and the television was on. Matthew's opinion had been by-passed as if he no longer had any say in this household. "Paddington!" came the gleeful cry. "Mummy lets me watch this."

Matthew trudged through to the kitchen. He felt trampled on, taken over, as if he was no longer in control. He was ruled by the ricocheting effect of my pain.

Upstairs, I could not settle. I was no longer resting, except physically. My mind was in turmoil. I could understand some of Matthew's pain and I wanted to help. I was sorry for him, yet also afraid of his anger. I knew he might fly at someone – maybe at the children, maybe at me. I knew it would not be meant personally if he did. Just as I sometimes have to bear more physical pain than I feel able, now he was bearing too much emotional pain.

Does it seem ungrateful of Matthew to be burdened by others' help? Therein lies yet another source of tension for him. He knows he ought to be grateful to others for all help offered. He would hate to hurt them by suggesting that their goodwill could be better channelled. So he bears more. Silently.

Inevitably, he feels a reaction. I want him to be free to express his reaction, and not to try to suppress everything, bottling up his feelings inside himself. He's inclined to do that anyway, having been taught at boarding school that it is "good" not to show unpleasant emotions. So strongly has this been ingrained in him that he automatically feels guilty when he finds anger within himself. At that stage he either denies it, or falls silent (easily mistaken for moodiness) as he tussles within himself.

On the one hand, Matthew wants to weep for me and shout out against the apparent injustice that he should see me suffer more than many others; on the other hand, he has this strong inbuilt sense that he should be able to cope. This is reinforced whenever he recognizes God's hand at work within all our suffering. If God is so clearly in it, then surely Matthew should be able to come through with a glowing Christian serenity?

And across the two threads, he has the practical everyday chores during my crises, such as keeping the children happy and finding the next meal – things which he is not accustomed to handling simultaneously.

One of the ways in which other people help us to endure with patience is by encouraging us in every way, including in prayer. Not the insistent kind of prayer which tells God what to do, but the quiet waiting upon him together. I was helped not only by the direct effect of prayer on myself, but also because I could see how much Matthew was strengthened and made more peaceful by it.

Every Monday for about 18 months while Matthew was at theological college, about a dozen friends joined together to pray. They were precipitated into meeting like this in 1980 while I was so critically ill, but they did not give up as soon as the crisis had passed. Even other very worthwhile demands on their time did not make them cease. For Matthew and myself, their faithfulness was an enormous encouragement. For themselves, they became convinced that those who pray benefit as much as the one being prayed for.

There was one such evening, just before Easter 1980, when the group was drawn to one particular verse which has continued to be a great source of strength. They had been silent for a long time as they simply lifted me to God in their minds. A stillness came upon them, gentle yet powerful. Then the quietness was broken by three different people.

"I've a tune repeating itself over and over in my ears," said Peter.

"I've a picture in my mind," said Anne.

"I've a verse which I cannot get out of my head," was John's contribution. "But I'm not sure where to find it."

"Maybe someone else will know?" Alastair was leading that evening. "Tell us what it is."

The words came easily as John spoke the verse: "The steadfast love of the Lord never ceases; his mercies never come to an end." Little could he guess how much his trust in those words would be tested the following years, with the long and continuing illness of his wife, Sadie.

"That's amazing that you should quote that verse!" exclaimed Peter. "Because the tune which came to me was from the song with those very words; they come from Lamentations 3." He picked up his guitar and everyone joined in quietly to sing the song about God's steadfast love.

After it was finished, it was Anne's turn. "The picture in my mind fits in with both the verse and the song," she said. "I can see a crocus, a beautiful crocus. The outer leaves are curled around the fragile petals of the flower. It's like loving hands protecting something, or someone, very precious."

The room was silent again while everyone reflected on what had been shared. They all marvelled at the one message of assurance and love, given so clearly in three different ways, but at the same time. Gradually the hush became diffused with praise, in prayer and in song, that God's Spirit should so graciously be among them.

I had been too tired to go to this particular meeting, but as soon as Matthew returned to me later in hospital I could see that he was radiant. He was filled and surrounded by an aura of peace, not a passive "Let happen what will happen", but a peace which was somehow very powerful.

The group did not quote this verse glibly, as a quick means of explaining the pain away without entering into our suffering. The words were actually written by Jeremiah among shouts of anguish to the Lord, "He [God] has driven me away and made me walk in darkness rather than light" (Lamentations 3:2). Yet Jeremiah's hope returned whenever he remembered that God's steadfast love remained even in the depths of suffering. "Though he brings grief, he will show compassion . . . " (Lamentations 3:32).

When my own trust crumbles and questioning slides into doubt, it is not only my physical strength which fails. I weaken emotionally and spiritually, too, and depend on others' help. Even though I was not there myself, that special evening in 1980 gave me a profound trust in God's steadfast love – no matter what. Through others waiting on God, as if on my behalf, I feel that Lamentations 3 is a special source of comfort.

In order to keep the significance of this verse alive within me, I must be patient. To look ahead is to lose patience. To look for a time-limit is to lose patience. To demand an explanation of God's purpose through it all is to lose patience. I have had to learn how to grit my teeth and force myself to get through. But that is not the sort of patience that God wants for me. He wants me to learn patience with joy.

I remember reading the book of Colossians while feeding our second baby. Because I was then caring for the two children, time was short and I was trying to cram my prayer time and Bible-reading into the brief peacefulness when one child was at playgroup. The sun streamed into our quiet sitting-room, almost as a picture of God's presence illumining what I was reading.

It was the first time that I had noticed the phrase, "patience with joy" (Colossians 1:11, RSV). That was part of Paul's prayer for the Christians he was addressing.

"Oooh, Lord," I prayed spontaneously, as soon as I noticed the three words. "I'd like patience with joy." I realized that, a lot of the time, my so-called "patience" was more like long-suffering; that I lacked the joy that comes from God's true patience. "Please give me patience with joy," I prayed.

I stopped for a moment. I did not hear God's physical

voice, but in the pause after my prayer a new thought came to me. It was as if God were talking to me.

"Patience and joy are not gifts. They are fruit, part of the fruit of the Holy Spirit. They grow slowly and surely like fruit on a tree. They cannot be stuck on with glue."

My momentary excitement waned a little. I realized that my prayer for patience and joy as a gift had been inappropriate. If I wanted those attributes, I had to be prepared to steep myself more fully in God's Spirit, so that the fruit would be a natural consequence of my life in him.

I adjusted my prayer. "Help me to live more closely to you – more in you than with you . . . And I'll still look to you to make patience and joy grow out of my life."

I felt quite subdued as I acknowledged what my prayer actually meant. Patience grows from endurance; endurance grows from suffering. To pray for patience was very different from praying for the pain to end. It meant opening myself to God, whether or not the pain continued. Indeed it meant accepting the possibility that the pain could continue, in order to bear fruit – God's fruit.

There would be no easy path to joy, either. To some extent, joy grows out of sorrow. To ask for the fruit of the Holy Spirit to be seen in my life was to accept God's hand completely. In his great wisdom he seems to have chosen to teach me his path to joy through suffering.

It seemed, and still does seem, to be a daunting road. I only keep on the apparently endless trudge of carrying on, by being encouraged. I need to be affirmed that I am in the Lord's hands, even when it looks as if he has let go of me.

To endure with patience sounds tremendously heroic; in reality it is tough and unexciting. Trapped in the midst of the pain, I am unable to stand back and look at my life objectively in the way that onlookers can. To endure patiently seems so endlessly hard; it drives me even to the point of despair.

It is paradoxical that, when I have felt thus, God has been reflected in me. I greatly value the comments of those friends whose perspective is different from my own. Elaine's words are but one example. She wrote, "Your courage and trust in the face of such suffering and ongoing discouragement cannot help but witness to the glory of God."

In the face of all that I have to endure, this is my encouragement. I can be a light to those around me. I can please God within my suffering. I can even have a ministry in suffering.

One letter that I will always treasure is from Geoff, who came to see me when I felt weary and spent. I had no idea at the time that I had anything to offer in life, to God or to others. Such a knowledge would have been sufficient encouragement for me to stop feeling so low and useless. Yet Geoff wrote:

> Thank you so much for our time together which gave me so much. It is a joy to be with you, and to see maybe something which you cannot: the quiet joy of Christ radiating through the daily painful and victorious cross that he has placed upon your frail shoulders. You may not see this "quiet joy" that I mention, but I can see it and have seen it before . . . Christ lives within you, and what we see in you is an unending limit of endurance and faithfulness which is possible only in him.

We can be very slow to encourage one another, yet each person who suffers desperately needs to be encouraged. He or she needs to know that, although many of the actions in life are completely curtailed by pain, his or her life is bearing fruit. It is worthwhile. It is the beginning of the journey towards healing through pain.

CHAPTER NINE

THERE IS MORE . . .

Since this book was first published I have continued bumping along, twice needing more major surgery but more frequently being admitted to hospital to be given more conservative care. The problem now is not primarily one of infection, but an inflammatory process. Because I have had so many major operations, bits of my abdomen have stuck together, forming adhesions. Thus, instead of everything moving about freely as normal, movement causes pain because the adhesions get tugged. This causes soreness, more superficial than pain. At times, however, the situation can become more threatening. The adhesions can twist, causing an acute obstruction in my intestine. That is horrible, then, with acute pain and exhausting vomiting. On such occasions the hope is always that the twist will settle, but if it doesn't, then yet more surgery cannot be avoided.

I find this an uneasy waiting game on every such occasion. If the surgeon waits too long to operate, my intestine could rupture, with potentially fatal results. If he were too hasty, I would be subjected to further major surgery with its nasty risks and consequences. As a result of living with that knowledge year after year, I am acutely aware of the fragility of life in general, and my own life in particular.

I began to write my own form of psalms, or letters to God.[1] Concentration during bad phases is often short-lived; so too are my written prayers. They are starkly honest. I felt I had nothing to offer to God, but I began to learn to offer even that. One such poem was written in bed in a lot of pain. I felt myself wince at every breath. I was caught between two impossible opposites: simultaneously longing for tenderness yet unable to let even Matthew close enough for me to receive just that.

> Do not kiss me now
> Do not come too close
> It's every breath which I must breathe
> Now
> and again
> Now . . .
>
> I hear a groan with each one:
> Is that my voice?
> I do not mean to grunt.
> If I hold my breath
> Does that help?
> . . . I cannot.
> My body's past such pride.
> Instead I'll delay each one . . .
>
> Just stroke me now:
> My arm
> My forehead
> Run your fingers through my hair.
> Without words

---

[1] These psalms were first published in *Faith in Flames* (Hodder & Stoughton, 1990), now out of print. All those quoted in this book may be found in *Treasures of Darkness* (Hodder & Stoughton, 1996).

Soothe me
Reach me
In this world with no words
this world where tears will not flow
for anguish.

Ah! Staccato stabbing
Pain piercing
Throbbing
Punctuated by these cries
Suppressed
but not silenced.

Would that this were singing
and not a cry of distress!
Oh my God! my God . . .

Accept each groan
each involuntary groan
and make it into
a song for you.

I did not hear my groaning as a song for God, nor, indeed,
my prayers. If I were honest, I was bored to hear them and
I wondered if God wasn't bored, too. However, I had no
choice. I either gave him all I could, or I hugged my hurts
to myself. I did not doubt his power to transform, and I discovered, with utter relief, that if I did truly lean the whole
of my trust on him, then he would bring some hope to my
despair. Certainly I found that, instead of these being
moments of my reaching out to God, the dynamic was in
fact his reaching out to me.

   This may sound rather grand; to me it felt pitiful. Yes, I
was aware of my relationship with God plumbing greater
depths and for that I was thankful; but even that spiritual
"reward" did not seem worth the cost. I am aware that this

sounds selfish, but I could barely see the worth in what was happening: not in my pain, nor my writing, nor even in God's gift of hope. As far as I was concerned, God was too late. He had allowed my body to be so damaged that my life was marred by a score running right through it. Others are quick to point out to me the truth of St Paul's words, "Now I know in part . . . " (1 Corinthians 13, verse 12). I quite concede that I cannot see the whole truth, but only a part of it. St Paul's verse ends, "Then I shall know fully, even as I am fully known." To me that is a hope in which I determine to trust but which I cannot quite believe; it feels akin to wishful thinking.

One springtime, a very ordinary scene from my window seemed to depict a parable of this very situation.

I was sitting very comfortably, gazing out to the three huge beech trees which stood majestically on the far side of our garden wall. The sun had risen quite high, and against its silvery brightness some dark rooks were silhouetted, black and menacing.

"Those rooks are terribly destructive," I remarked to Matthew as he came through. "Look at them! They're pulling those poor trees to pieces."

As we watched, no fewer than four rooks worked on different parts of the trees. They pecked with their beaks and stamped with their feet, clawing determinedly at the twigs until they had cut off the piece they wanted. Some of the twigs seemed enormous, and I was amazed the birds were able to fly at all carrying such cumbersome pieces.

Matthew was more philosophical than I. "I was just thinking how clever it all is," he mused. "If you look carefully, they only take the bits which come off easily. It's a very neat way of removing the weak parts of the tree, which actually has the effect of keeping the whole thing growing more strongly."

He was right.

And that was only a part of the whole picture. The rooks were not purposeless. Their tearing-down was not futile. Elsewhere, of course, they were building their nests. But the trees where the new nests were being built, although only half a mile away, were out of my sight. From where I was sitting, I could see only the destructive tearing-down.

That morning I knew how easy it was – and is – to mourn when we see tearing-down; to fail to see that that is part of building. It cannot, or should not, be separated from building-up. For without the tearing-down of twigs there would be no building of nests.

This is why I remained uncomfortable talking or writing about the destructive element of suffering. We may feel only brokenness; we may never see what is being built up. But that does not – or should not! – matter. Indeed, I knew that, just as the rooks' new nests were not even in the same tree as these ones where twigs were being torn off, perhaps the harvest from my pain might never be visible in my life here, but it could yet be to come. Or perhaps others could see what I could not.

I wrote many more psalms. In the small hours of the morning I poured out my soul before God – and once again, it was as if God was pouring out his prayer as a weapon. Prayer is, instead, more like a window – a window to myself, and a window to God.

Gradually, gradually, prayer became less of an event in my day and more of a pair of spectacles which changed the colour and hue of every part of life. It was less of a quest for God to involve himself more actively in me; more of a means for me to learn how to involve myself more actively in him.

Perhaps I make life sound as if I have learned by now . . . learned to "cope", whatever that may mean. But I'm afraid I haven't. I may be on my way but I haven't arrived. I can only say that I am still journeying. I know that I haven't arrived because I can see my reaction whenever I wake up, say, with overwhelming nausea and I realize that I face another difficult day. My first reaction is not so much a prayer but more a cry, a panic, a scream: "Take it away!"

And God hasn't. He could, but he hasn't. He doesn't always necessarily do what we ask, or tell him to do. We can rely upon the fact that he is who he says he is but we cannot insist that he give us his gifts. That is not his promise. The promise God repeated over and over again to every person to whom he spoke is consistent: "I will be with you." Indeed, Jesus used the present tense as well as the future: "I *am* with you." His very name, Emmanuel, means, "God with us".

Since the beginning of time our God is one who comes searching for us. He comes "walking in the garden in the cool of the day", calling, "Where are you?" (Genesis 3, verse 8–9). Whether we hide from him, as did Adam and Eve, or feel angry with him, as did Cain in the next chapter of Genesis, God still comes calling for us, asking us to respond to him. Whether we are silently ashamed or remain truculently argumentative, the God who made us loves us so faithfully that he cannot help but continue his search for us. He calls out to us: "Where are you?" or "What are you doing?"

Do I reply?

Will I?

Or do I, like Adam, attempt to cover, quickly, and hide whatever causes me to cringe in shame? Or shall I, like Cain, hug my hurt to myself and let the resentment fester?

God is a God of love. He comes to heal, not to destroy. His plans are for good, not evil. When he comes, he brings peace.

Yet we are caught in our humanity and, certainly if I speak only for myself, God's presence alone does not always seem sufficient. I take comfort that I am not alone, for I read that the disciples were likewise dismayed when Jesus, though present, didn't "do something!" They had the benefit of *seeing* him with their own eyes, yet still that was not enough for them. When life became rough and they found themselves in the midst of a storm, (Matthew 8; Mark 4; Luke 8), Jesus was with them but (horror of horrors!) he had the temerity to *sleep* through their distress. They wanted to be rescued; in fact, they got into the awful cycle (one that, I confess, I also know rather well!) in which their fear led to desperation, and their desperation fed their fear. Eventually, in utter dismay, they went to Jesus where he slept with the sweet innocence of a baby. "Teacher, don't you *care* if we drown?" (italics mine; Mark 4, verse 38).

Why did Jesus sigh at their request for him to help? I once asked myself. Why did he condemn the disciples for having little faith when at least they had come to him?! What else could they have done? What other action was open to them, other than to shake Jesus from his divine oblivion?

The answer is embarrassingly straightforward. They could have stopped to think that, since Jesus was with them, they must be safe. Instead of panicking, they could have gone to see what he was doing. They could have imitated him and lain beside him through the storm. I write this tentatively because I know the enormity of the challenge. When I find myself caught by a storm, in the middle of a squall with the wind howling and the waves breaking over my boat, the easiest option is to cry for God to save me. Far harder is it to look for where he is and, if he is calmly sleeping, to lie down beside him with my own head on his chest. Yet I am now convinced that that is the way towards real peace and true healing.

Oh, how often have I thought those same words of accusation in my heart, but not dared to utter them! "Teacher, don't you care?" Has God not *seen* my (our) stormy troubles? How *can* he sleep through them? After all, we do not have whatever heavenly qualities Jesus had that enabled him to sleep so peacefully in that boat: we humans have to contend with the realistic fear that we might die!

We have the answer to these questions as well. We may not like them: the truth can hurt. But we have been told, unequivocally, that God does care. The fact is that he does see and know; of course he does. He does understand how badly storms rage. But he knows something else as well. He knows a peace that is profound enough to carry him through the most violent storm. Jesus knew how to take rest, no matter what was happening. And there's more: he invites us to receive exactly the same gift as he was enjoying.

That, I think, is why Jesus answered the disciples with a slight sigh. How long would they take to hear what he had offered them? Had they not even heard yet? Would they not respond to his invitation? God can give something greater to whoever looks for him, the Giver, more than for his miracles.

Jesus offers us peace during our storms, a peace within that is as profound a miracle as if he were to rescue us. We can have what he was having. What it does take – and I do not write this lightly – is for us to watch him and to listen.

We have an outrageous God. He comes to us where we feel uncomfortable and then, to our astonishment, he announces that this is where he'd like to make his home.

He has come to me in the very places that I wish did not exist. He has come to the centre of my trauma and pain; to the middle of all that I want to forget; the place from which I wish to escape; the place I have tried hard to deny or cover up. And there he says, shockingly, "This is where I want to make my home. May I come and dwell with you here?" I find this to be a mind-boggling request! He wants to dwell with me where I am – not somewhere else. He wants me as I am – not as somebody else. Always, always, he begins here, not there. He begins now, not then.

And God does not merely visit. He stays. He has come and stayed with me because he knows his presence transforms any place. His presence consecrates it. He makes it holy. Well, he is the one who makes *us* holy!

And then, as if he had not astonished me enough, God began to turn his attention to work on the things that I wanted to sweep under the carpet. "Hush," he has whispered quietly to my noisy protestations. "I am a carpenter. I'm a potter. My craft is creation and re-creation!" And here I am, quietened because he is working on the very places from which I used to wait for him to take me away. I used to ask him to "heal" my awful memories of the bad times and the grim times, and I meant "rid me of them!" I have asked him how I'm supposed to live in such a broken body. What a surprise to hear him whisper that he wants me to love deeply.

"Love as I love," God says.

Love, not reject.

This call to love was reinforced in a totally practical way by my doctor, who astonished me recently by her challenge. She sat by my bed, calm and unflustered, while I lay feeling sick, sweaty and far from calm. I loathe feeling sick and I therefore hated the whole situation . . . Ugh, I felt so trapped, and I could not run away.

"Jane," she said. "Are you forgetting how tenderly God looks upon you? . . . He loves you, Jane: the whole of you, including your body. And he longs for each of us to love, too. He asks us to love whatever and whomever he loves."

What, when I was *vomiting*? How could I love my body when it was letting me down as it was?

"No, Jane," persisted my doctor. "Your body is not letting you down. She is being faithful to you. She is giving expression to you. She is part of you . . . She IS you!"

How can I love what I hate? The only answer I can give,

at this stage along my unfinished pathway, is that I have glimpsed how God looks upon me. So far I have not reached the goal, although I've seen it set before me. So far the only route I know is to seek to obey his command to "Love your enemies". At the moment I still think of my body as my enemy. If I learn to love it as my enemy, then that will be step one, I believe. Once I have taken that step, I presume that she will no longer be my enemy but my friend. I am learning, and I am trying, although paradoxically God's way is less like trying and more like listening to him. That brings me back to his invitation for me to lay my head upon his breast, and listen. He says that I am his friend: will I ponder that? If he calls me friend, and I insist that my body is my enemy, then do I consider my opinion greater than his? He says that I am precious, and honoured in his sight, and he loves me. He speaks so very gently, I know if only I would come to him and rest with him, I would then hear his words to be much less as "commands" and much, much more as the gentle, tender soothing he intends for his children.

He knows all our suffering, our every experience including all the painful, difficult ones. And he says that they are central to the fabric of our being. More than that, he declares that they are too precious to forget. He holds pain along with us, close to his heart, and he will not let us go. This I am coming to know truly and to picture, at last, how he can comfort. I am coming to rely on him to be prepared to continue to soothe me for the rest of time, if necessary, or for every time I ever need to be comforted . . . he is here. This is healing deeper than I might ever have imagined, just as we read: "[He] is able to do immeasurably more than all we ask or imagine, according to his power that is at work within us . . . " (Ephesians 3, verse 20). Healing is very, very different from cure.

If we confine "healing" to being freedom from what we

find unpleasant, then we may be cutting ourselves off from encountering and embracing the profound depths of God.

It would be foolish for Matthew or myself to forget that my symptoms can return any time. Medically this would be no surprise. It is easy for us to give thanks to God when he gives us newfound strength. I am learning, somewhat hesitantly, to thank him also for my weakness. To do otherwise is to acknowledge only half of what God is doing in our lives. To "put the pain years all behind", as some people urge, is a way of disregarding some very precious truths about him. I want to resist the so-called optimism which empties my experience of its awfulness. I believe God does not confine himself to areas where he is recognized – in visible healing. He is with us in our pain as much as he is in our rejoicing. His light shines in our darkness as well as in our day. The place from which we want to escape may be the very place where he is waiting to be found. When we have lost sight of him altogether we fear him to have withdrawn; in fact he has embedded himself in the darkness within us where we fear even to look.

In a subtle way, rejoicing can be a way of dismissing pain, and I believe that by avoiding pain we can avoid healing. We cannot speak of healing if we will not speak of pain. Our Lord carried his scars into his resurrection.

Thus I wrote, in another of my psalms:[2]

> There's a score across the sky, there
> Where an aeroplane's just been
> Cutting it and marring it
> Slicing it in two
>
> There's a score across my abdomen
> Where surgeons' knives have been

---

[2] ibid.

Cutting me and marring me
Slicing me in two

There's a score across my life, Lord
Where deepest hurts have been
I am so marred
and cut apart
in many, many ways

That trail above me's fading now
Blown across the sky
The scar across my abdomen
is fading with the years
But the scar across my life, Lord,
Never can be swept away

Save me from seeing only hurt:
Show me your hand as well.
For with one touch
You leave your mark
Changing me, not marring me
Leading me
to you.